# Tongue Shakers

*Interviews and Narratives on Speaking Mother Tongue in a Multicultural Society*

Margie Shaheed

**Hamilton Books**

An Imprint of
Rowman & Littlefield
Lanham • Boulder • New York • Toronto • Plymouth, UK

**Copyright © 2017 by Hamilton Books**
4501 Forbes Boulevard, Suite 200, Lanham, Maryland 20706
Hamilton Books Acquisitions Department (301) 459-3366

Unit A, Whitacre Mews, 26-34 Stannary Street,
London SE11 4AB, United Kingdom

All rights reserved
Printed in the United States of America
British Library Cataloguing in Publication Information Available

Library of Congress Control Number: 2016940153
ISBN: 978-0-7618-6805-7 (pbk : alk. paper)—ISBN: 978-0-7618-6806-4 (electronic)

Cover art by James J. Polacci and Denise Polacci DePalma.

∞™ The paper used in this publication meets the minimum requirements of American National Standard for Information Sciences Permanence of Paper for Printed Library Materials, ANSI/NISO Z39.48-1992.

I dedicate this book to my grandsons
Yusef, Halim, Nasir, Achilles and Jabari (in memoriam)
for giving the world and me hope;

to Stanford Lewis for loving me
and teaching me how to be a wild cat;

and to Askia Toure for leading the way.

"Some folks is born wid they feet on de sun
and they kin seek out de inside meanin' of words."

—Zora Neale Hurston

# Contents

| | |
|---|---|
| Acknowledgments | ix |
| Introduction | 1 |
| Section 1 Mother Tongue Coming to America | 15 |
|     Living through the Bosnian War | 15 |
|     ESL Classes Brings Friendship to a Little Boy | 17 |
|     Africa at the Center | 19 |
|     Braiding a Path to Entrepreneurship | 20 |
|     From Doctor to Translator | 20 |
|     Learning English in Exile | 21 |
|     Back to Africa | 23 |
|     There's No Place Like Home | 23 |
|     Speaking English and Driving Fast | 26 |
|     The American Myth: Seeing Is Believing | 27 |
|     Mother and Daughter Interview | 28 |
|     I Can't Talk to My Grandmother | 32 |
|     Ethiopian at Heart | 33 |
|     The Road to English Is Long | 34 |
|     Learning by Watching | 35 |
|     Forever Mother Tongue | 38 |
|     Americans Help Me Speak English | 39 |
|     Translating for Love | 40 |
|     From Rome with Love | 41 |
|     Speaking Fulani, Connecting to Heritage | 42 |
|     Patois from the Island of Jamaica | 43 |
|     Coming to America | 45 |
|     Salsa in the Afternoon | 48 |

|  |  |
|---|---|
| America Here I Am | 49 |
| Blacks Speak Spanish Too | 51 |
| Beating the Odds | 55 |

### Section 2 Mother Tongue American Style — 59
| | |
|---|---|
| The Culture Bearer | 59 |
| Spanish American Style | 62 |
| A Work in Progress | 64 |
| A Honduran Bronx Tale | 66 |
| Blacxicana | 70 |

### Section 3 Black English as Mother Tongue: Black in the Day — 73
| | |
|---|---|
| A Perspective on African-American Language | 73 |
| Code Switching: A Tool for Survival | 75 |
| If Black English Isn't a Language, Then Tell Me, What Is?* | 78 |
| We Be Speakin' | 80 |
| Creole Missed Me, Black English Found Me | 81 |
| From Black English to Slang to Mandarin | 82 |

### Appendix A: Poems — 85
| | |
|---|---|
| Code Breakers & Tongue Shakers | 85 |
| Chakras of Refugee Embodiment or 7 Ways to Love Your Asian Body by Tu Anh Phan | 87 |
| ESL by Anonymous | 89 |

### Appendix B: Interview Questionnaire Guides — 93
| | |
|---|---|
| Interview Questionnaire Guide (Black English) | 94 |

| | |
|---|---|
| References | 95 |
| Index | 97 |

# Acknowledgments

This book would not be possible if it were not for all of the individuals who allowed me to interview them for this project. I thank them for trusting me, giving me access, and for teaching me so much. I spent hours in the library requesting research materials and using public access computers and study rooms to do my writing and transcribing of tapes. In this regard, I would like to take this opportunity to thank the staff of the Memphis Public Library (Whitehaven branch) and the staff of the East Cleveland Public Library for graciously honoring my many requests and creating an environment conducive to getting my work done.

As the project progressed it became necessary for me to travel. I would like to acknowledge and thank the following individuals for contributing funds which enabled me to take a research trip to Houston, Texas to interview the Valencia family: Dr. Nancy Gerber, Janet Minnieweather, Donna Carrigano, Alberta Drake, Aldo and Anna Tambellini, Lori Johnson, DJ Tony Motley, Lori Jackson, Steven Metoyer, James Polacci, Adrienne Metoyer, Lorraine Currelley, Shirley Nelson, Charlene Fix, Sherlynn Allen-Harris, Gry Hala, Dr. Voris Glasper and Vince Robinson.

I am truly indebted to my inner circle of mentors, intellectuals and scholars who stimulate and challenge my thinking. Foremost, I would like to thank Stanford Lewis for his unfaltering support 24/7 and for being the resident scholar; Dr. Mary E. Weems for reading my manuscript and giving me sound scholarly advice; Askia Toure for being the standard; and finally, I thank Dr. Nancy Gerber, my former Rutgers professor, for reading and editing my manuscript, and for standing with me over the years, believing in my work, even when I did not—I am forever your student.

# Introduction

*Tongue Shakers: Interviews and Narratives on Speaking Mother Tongue in a Multicultural Society* is a book exploring the lives of immigrants, Americans born into immigrant families, and African Americans on the topic of speaking mother tongue in America's multicultural society. I was curious to know the challenges people faced as speakers of a language other than English in a society where English dominates. Although constitutionally the United States has no national official language, American English has been the de facto official language for over 240 years. I have included African Americans in this project as well because "even though blacks have embraced English as their native tongue, still the African cultural set persists, that is, a predisposition to imbue the English word with the same sense of value and commitment . . . accorded African culture." (Smitherman, 1977 p. 79)

My work continues in the tradition of the work of Zora Neale Hurston (1901-1960), African-American novelist, dramatist and cultural anthropologist. *Mules and Men,* which remains her primary expression of the extensive anthropological research and collecting of folktales (1927-1932) was not published until 1935. "Its publication was historically important, the first book of Afro-American folklore collected by a black American to be presented by a major publisher for a general reading audience." (Hemenway, 1978, p. xviii) Although it was considered an "unscientific work" by scholars such as Franz Boas, it was believed it would have value as a reference book. Hurston's writing technique "falls somewhere between scientific reporting and personal journalism, producing a repeated pattern of experience." (Hemenway, 1978, 167) Hurston's unique contribution validates Black speech as a serious form of spoken expression worthy of study and preservation.

I first became inspired by Hurston's work while taking undergraduate courses at Fordham University and Rutgers University in cultural anthropology and English with a concentration in writing. While studying both disciplines I was confronted with the genius of Hurston—*Mules and Men* in anthropology and *Their Eyes Were Watching God* in African-American literature. What struck me most about Hurston's work was that she defied tradition refusing to separate from ordinary people choosing to study her own culture from the inside out. She was motivated in such a way that she went out and did the field work, the first African-American woman to do so. In this regard it's important to note that Hurston performed this work reserved for graduate students of anthropology without having first earned a graduate degree although a scholarship enabled her to enter Barnard College, where she received her B.A. in 1928.

Concerned with the history and condition of Black Americans Hurston spent her lifetime writing about rural southern Blacks because it was the world she knew best. Although my inquiry includes multicultural perspectives, my work, like Hurston's, captures and honors the spoken language of ordinary people as told in their own words without the restraints and rigor of the academy. One of my mentors, Dr. Mary E. Weems, calls me an "intercultural global anthropologist."

Hurston was working at a time when the United States was segregated, which some could say worked to her advantage because she had access to the brightest Black minds and scholarship of the time. At Howard University faculty included E. Franklin Frazier, Alain Locke, and Carter G. Woodson. She was awarded a research fellowship from Carter G. Woodson who was the leading Black historian in America, which enabled her to leave New York City in late February of 1927 to collect folktales in her hometown of Eatonville, Florida. During her expedition she reported to and consulted with Woodson on a regular basis. As well, she had other brilliant Black minds to confer with such as W.E.B. Du Bois, who ultimately proved to be the intellectual godfather of the Harlem Renaissance, and she received scholarly guidance from her former professor at Howard University, Rhodes Scholar, Alain Locke.

Hurston's positive relationship with Black scholars does not in any way diminish the positive student/professor/mentor relationship she had with white anthropologist Franz Boas in spite of segregation. To the contrary, her undergraduate studies with him at Columbia University legitimized her work as an anthropologist and proved to be instrumental in developing the required discipline essential to becoming a serious writer and a respected social scientist. Hurston made important discoveries about her own culture namely that it was something worthy of scholarly study. At the time, Franz Boas was the foremost anthropologist in the country in this branch of social science in its infancy stages. In a personal letter to Boas requesting that he write the introduction to *Mules and Men* Hurston writes, "So I hope that the unscientific matter that must be there for the sake of the average reader will not keep you from writing the introduction" (Hemenway 1978, p. 163-164). Boas granted her request only "after checking the manuscript for authenticity" (164).

*Tongue Shakers* is written for general audiences and the average reader. I, too, have been most fortunate to count scholars and intellectuals, including those from my time at Rutgers University as friends and mentors who have stimulated me and steered me in the right direction. Dr. Nancy Gerber, my former professor, regularly reads and edits my manuscripts, and as always my mentors give me useful comments and professional advice. I also share Zora's profession as a creative writer. I have published poems and short stories in literary journals and I have three chapbooks of poetry in print.

I began interviewing people for this project three years ago. I have interviewed 100 individuals from urban neighborhoods located in the American South (Memphis and Ft. Meyers), Midwest (Cleveland), West (Houston) and East Coast (Newark, New York, Washington D.C. and Boston). Interviews from 37 of these people are presented in *Tongue Shakers* 14 men and 23 women ages 16 to 81 years old. The experience for me has been rewarding and a journey of discovery. I found people to interview as I normally went about my day. I started the practice of carrying my tape recorder, camera, notebook, questions and release forms with me daily so that I would be prepared at any moment to conduct an interview. If I heard someone speaking in an accent I would politely approach them and introduce myself as a writer working on an exciting project. I explained my project to them and asked if I could interview them. For the most part my narrators have been strangers whom I have encountered on the city streets of America. In some cases I was granted an interview on the spot so if this happened we found a quiet place like a coffee shop, park or the library to do the interview. At other times I may have caught someone who was on their way to work or trying to make another appointment, so we exchanged telephone numbers and arranged to meet at a later time, usually at a public place in the city.

Once the project was well underway I took several trips for the purpose of interviewing people. I found people on the East Coast to be more receptive and willing to talk me about themselves. People in the South were more apprehensive. All of my trips proved fruitful and I am still amazed at all of the people who let me interview them for this project. Of all of my trips the one to Houston stands out. It was hosted by the Valencia family who immigrated to the United States from Colombia in the early 1960s. My contact for the family was the daughter Vilma. She invited me to stay for one week in the home she shares with the family's matriarch her eighty-one year old mother Jesusita Valencia. I had the opportunity to meet and interview Vilma's siblings Myriam, George and Harold as well.

Vilma's father, Jorge Valencia died in 2014 but his presence is felt through an altar of family pictures in the small room adjacent to the living room. Upon meeting for the first time Mrs. Valencia gave me a great big hug and kiss. I immediately felt comfortable. Their home, which is beautifully furnished with Italian handcrafted furniture, features lovely drapes hand sewn by Mrs. Valencia who is a seamstress by trade. She has a serious green thumb too, because plants adorn the rooms. Spanish language television, radio and Latin music are heard throughout the house at all times. During my stay Mrs. Valencia kept urging me to listen to the news in English. I refused because I wanted to keep the environment as natural as possible and I wanted to experience Spanish in a way in which I hadn't already.

I learned from my interviews with this family that the Valencias insisted their children speak Spanish only in the home while they were growing up in America, a place that seems at times to promote the idea that we should all speak the same language. George Valencia (Vilma's oldest brother) gave the example that when he was a little boy if he wanted to ask his parents for a quarter to buy candy he had better do it in Spanish if he wanted positive results. This practice of retaining the mother tongue in the home forged a strong cultural identity and instilled pride in the Valencia children. This family lived a truly bilingual existence in this multicultural society.

What resonates with me about this family is that they had an equal commitment to the culture they left behind and the new culture they were entering. They left South America because of the father's inability to find lucrative employment in Colombia's depressed steel industry. In America, he could use his skills as an engineer, which guaranteed his ability to provide for his family (which incidentally was a requirement for him to enter America). In America, the Valencia family established themselves as homeowners, small business owners, educators, public servants, i.e. police and military, and many would maintain that they have achieved the American dream. It was inspiring and a pleasure to meet this family. I was there to work but Vilma and her mother made me feel like I was visiting with long time friends. The Valencia interviews are located at the end of Section 1 and I have included photos of the family.

This project has taken many shapes. The thought first came to me about ten years ago when I wrote a poem about my mother called *Code Breakers*. The poem speaks about how my mother was the person in the community who was sought after by our neighbors to read and to explain difficult terms containing riddled codes in their important papers. Often during these sessions in our living room my mother would fill out cumbersome forms and was entrusted to counsel our neighbors on their personal affairs. We represented the changing face of a southeast Cleveland, Ohio, neighborhood that was witnessing white flight to the suburbs in the late 1960s.

My mother experienced a windfall when her estranged husband died suddenly and she became eligible for his veteran's widow benefits. She took the lump sum of money and bought a house because she believed that becoming a homeowner would translate into stability for her family and that we would have a better life. This was a new working class redlined Black neighborhood. Redlining refers to discrimination by banks, mortgage companies and realtors against people who are poor. A common practice is to withhold loans on property that is considered located in better neighborhoods. Instead, these companies steer poor and Black buyers to a particular neighborhood, creating racially segregated and poor communities.

Fast forward, I was invited to submit work to *Mom Egg Review* for its spring 2013 issue on the theme of mother tongue. Since I had no existing unpublished work on the subject it was necessary for me to generate new material. I revisited the Code Breakers theme because I saw it as being closely related to mother tongue in that in both instances it includes people who struggle with the use of language. I conceived the idea that I would interview a couple of women who spoke a language other than English. Since I am a poet I decided to write poems from the story that would unfold from their interviews. I started paying close attention to the people I encountered on my daily travels and throughout my neighborhood. I don't own a car so I have an opportunity to engage with strangers on an up close and personal level.

My first interview was at the McDonald's several blocks from my home with a woman from the Philippines. After I explained my project to her she agreed to be interviewed on the spot. I was nervous. I plunged in since at the time I had not prepared interview questions. On this summer day she wore a pretty flower print sun dress and a floppy hat covering hair that ran slightly past her shoulders. Although she stood out because she looked different she was very much a part of my all Black neighborhood. She can be seen on any given day walking her two small daughters to nursery school. She is a stay at home mom, and her husband, who is African-American, supports the family.

My second interview was with an Ethiopian woman, a business executive whom I approached for an interview at a popular coffee shop while she was there with her husband and two children. I heard her speak to her children in her mother tongue and I knew I had to interview her. She and I had an interview three weeks later. I found both women to be open and honest as each shared their unique stories of wrestling with a language that is not their mother tongue. The greatest challenge faced by both women was teaching their American born children to speak their first language in an environment where they have very little support and few opportunities to speak it on a regular basis except for at home.

Both women were most concerned that their children have the ability to speak their mother tongue so that they can communicate effectively with relatives living in the country of origin. The two poems that came from these interviews were first published by *Mom Egg Review* under the title *Code Breakers & Tongue Shakers*. Since *Tongue Shakers* essentially grew out of these early poems, I am including them in the book in Appendix A which includes poems written by two other writers who were interviewed for this project. Please note that the names used in the "Code Breakers & Tongue Shakers" poems are pseudonyms; the author of the poem "ESL" wishes to remain anonymous.

This is not to say that all of my interviews went smoothly. I experienced many instances where people were suspicious of me and my motives and not so willing to talk. For instance, regularly people would agree to an interview and then when I called them at the appointed time they had changed their mind and would refuse to speak with me. In other cases folks granted me interviews but would refuse to give me their age or some other piece of personal information. They would begin asking questions about what I intended to do with their information. I tried to arrest their fears by explaining the project to them again. There were many times though when people I met felt comfortable and shared insightful stories about their lives and how they use language. It is these wonderful experiences that fill the pages of this book. I challenged myself further to create an atmosphere where the person would feel safe and comfortable enough with me to openly share their story.

I had decided since people were likely to change their mind if given time to think about it that I would start interviewing people on the spot while they still thought it was a good idea. On one such occasion I was in Shaker Square in Cleveland, Ohio, set up at Dewy's Coffee Shop, a magnet for people of diverse cultures and backgrounds. I was selling my chapbooks and recruiting people for interviews as they passed by my table on the sidewalk. I stopped a woman who told me she was born in India. Dressed in western clothes except for her bindi she was young, stout and short with a solitary long jet black braid running down the center of her back. I explained my project to her and she agreed to be interviewed. I offered her a seat at the table with me, which she refused. Not to be discouraged, I began asking my questions. She told me her first name was Kala, which means "bright" in her mother tongue. When I asked for her exact birthplace she hesitated and then said, "wait, I have to call my husband to ask him if I can talk to you." I said, "ok" and so I waited. She dialed her husband and spoke to him in her language, careful not to look at me. When I heard her say "bye" she informed me in heavily accented English that her husband would not allow her to talk to me. She apologized and left. I couldn't help but feel a sense of intense disappointment as I stared at the sheet of paper nearly blank except for her name—Kala—a little ray of brightness.

I stopped writing the poems because I felt as if I were missing the mark. In retrospect, I believe the anthropologist within me was stoked by those first interviews. It was at this moment that *Tongue Shakers* was born. I immediately changed my approach to reflect this new insight. I started educating myself on conducting qualitative research studies. I wanted to create some type of organizational structure in which to frame and present the interviews for the general reader. I scoured the internet for articles and I called my local university for textbook references. I read and read for months. And, as always, I consulted with my group of mentors, intellectuals and scholars who read my manuscript, edited my prospectus, and gave me scholarly direction. It is my hope that *Tongue Shakers* will have value as a reference book as does Hurston's *Mules & Men*.

I decided to conduct what are called semistructured interviews. This type of interview works well when you will have only one chance to interview the person. It uses an interview questionnaire guide, a set of questions that are asked in a particular order consistently with each person. It insures reliable, accurate and useful data. This type of interview, because of its open structure, allows room for the interviewer and narrator to follow new leads. (Bernard, 1995 p. 210) There are instances where I used the questionnaire as a written survey for people who I could not interview in person. The narrators who submitted written responses to the questionnaires were Jodi N., Madinah D., Harold V., Lorraine C., Myriam Q. and Mercy T. Also, it seemed only logical since African-Americans share the peculiar institution of enslavement and all of the historical and cultural implications that forced movement to the Americas produced warranted a different set of questions for narrators interviewed for the Black English section. The interview questionnaire guides are located in Appendix B.

There has been a shift in attitude about the relationship of interviewer to narrator. In the past, scholars in the social sciences have theorized the relationship between the person who is asking the questions (interviewer) and the person who yields answers (interviewee or respondent) as being one of unequal power. In this instance the person being interviewed is seen as passive and the interviewer as authoritative. However, if we look at what each brings to the table—the interviewer brings skill and knowledge based on research in the discipline; and the narrator (interviewee) brings the intimate knowledge of having lived the experience that is recounted and told, we see a relationship of equality. "The interviewer thus sees the work as a collaboration" (Yow, 2015, p. 1). For the course of this project I have adopted the term narrator to describe the person who is being interviewed. It is my goal to empower the storyteller for it is they who are providing the primary source material.

I conducted the interviews using a digital recorder so that I could capture every word, preserving ideas, concepts and insights shared by the narrator. I maintained a composition tablet of notes written while in the field and recorded my observations and reflections of the process. I then manually transcribed the tapes and compiled on my computer a file of unedited interview data. From there I made a decision to present the data as a first person narrative or in question and answer format. The determining factor as to narrative or question and answer had to do with the amount of autobiographical information contained in the responses. Using my writer's sensibility, which is unapologetically subjective and is contrary to the western myth of objectivity, because all human research is a product of subjectivity, if I *felt* there was enough detail and information contained in the interview for it to read like a story then I presented it as a narrative by removing the questions, reordering the responses and adding transitions. If the answers contained less detail or if it were the case where the narrator was not as proficient in English I presented those interviews in a question and answer format. I think including both formats breaks up the monotony of having one or the other throughout.

Once the interview was in its final draft form I sent the copy by email to the narrator so that they could read over what I had written and have the opportunity to correct or clarify any of the information. The interviews presented in this book are only minimally edited for readability in an effort to help the reader hear the narrator's beautiful voice as I might have experienced it in the actual interview. In most cases the real names of narrators are used except where noted with an asterisk.

When it came time to analyze the data I printed out copies of the transcripts and using a red pen I coded the data into loose categories around the issue of how mother tongue influences work, home, community and personal cultural identity. I looked for reoccurring themes, words, actions and feelings. For the majority of the narrators they answered similarly for some questions so it was possible to arrive at some generalizations. For instance, when asked if speaking English is important if you live and work in America most agreed that lack of fluency in American English puts immigrants at a disadvantage for hopes of achieving success and advancement in education and work. The same was true for African-Americans interviewed for this project. When asked what would cause narrators to lose his or her mother tongue most agreed that losing the ability to speak mother tongue in the multicultural society is a serious concern due to the tendency to speak English only. Consequently, it may lessen the narrator's ability to communicate in their mother tongue with family members living in the country of origin or perhaps with older members of the family living in America who may not speak English or who speak very little English.

My analysis is nontraditional as was Hurston's. I work from the perspective of *showing* what the interviews uncovered (which is really the purpose of this book) rather than discussing what the research found. In this respect, I would like to take a moment to share a few excerpts from the interviews that *caught my eye*. Tongue Shakers is divided into three sections:

*Section 1 – Mother Tongue Coming to America –* This section of the book features interviews with individuals who have immigrated to the United States or who have visited from other countries. The Center for Immigration Studies reports that there are 61 million immigrants and their young children now living in the United States. The cultural landscape widens. People bring their customs, beliefs, and most of all their language with them. The human act of melding two worlds together can be a daunting task. Here are accounts from narrators describing their experiences with learning this new culture:

> Kamala: *I feel like I was born here as a new born because when a baby is born they don't know about the world. I have to learn everything about this country. I have to learn each and every thing. Even for the coins we used to say rupees. Different names for different things like penny. We know that it's money. The names of the things are different so we have to learn everything. That's why I feel like a new born baby here. I spent one year here [learning the language] now I feel like I'm crawling. [Laughter]*
>
> Amatoulaye: *So when I came here first it was in New York I had to learn to speak the language. I didn't know nothing [reflects] how to say hi or bye. Or even how to say open the door.*
>
> *Chen: *When I arrived in the United States I was confused because coming from a homogeneous society I grew up thinking the whole world look like me. We moved to Lexington, MA, in an all white community. I found going to school to be very hard because I couldn't speak the language and therefore I could not play with the other kids.*

These first-hand accounts provide commentary on starting from scratch. The analogy drawn to that of a baby mirrors the difficulties that can arise from learning a new language and culture. In spite of this many have managed to prevail and become citizens who successfully make a meaningful contribution to our greater society:

> Henry: *We have learned a lot in America. We know how to build careers and professions. I have a degree in business and engineering and my wife is pursuing her business degree.*

Some narrators have described it as a juggling act as they reveal challenges of having to fight the pressure to speak English only:

> Laure: *French is my first language and English is my second language. Because I have no shame concerning my background, I am not afraid to speak French in the presence of English speaking Americans. There is pressure from this society to speak English only.*

While a few narrators in this project believe this is our nation's pivotal source of power—one language uniting America making us stronger -- there are others, however, who believe this phenomenon of a dominant language in a multicultural society derails our access to other peoples and severs cultural ties among us:

> *Moussa: I think America is so big and vast it needs one language to stay united.*
>
> *Vilma: I think having the ability to speak more than one language has its advantages in a society where its citizens speak one dominant language because it allows me the freedom to access a variety of cultures and verbal expressions.*

*Section 2 – Mother Tongue American Style* - This section contains interviews with individuals who are Americans born into immigrant families; the last interview in this section is from a narrator born in Philadelphia, raised speaking English until age 9 when her family relocated to Puerto Rico forcing her to learn Spanish in order to navigate her new culture:

> *Tu: I call myself the 1.5 generation because even though I grew up in America my family is so Vietnamese making that a great part of my identity too.*

Some find themselves in the position of being forced to learn English only, causing the mother tongue to disappear, as a means to advance in work and education.

> *Anthony: My father told me that we were raised to speak English so that we could compete against the white person and the way to do that was to get educated so that we could compete in a white world. Being brown and Hispanic we looked different, we spoke different, we had a different culture, we ate different foods and they didn't believe we would have the same opportunities as whites if we were uneducated. We learned to read it, write it, and we learned to compete... I think it was a great injustice for my parents not to speak Spanish to us at home because it's always better to know two languages.*

There is great pressure for immigrants to assimilate and adopt the language and customs of the majority. On the other hand there are immigrants who desire and work toward assimilation:

> *Mercy: For my family members, knowing English was what made assimilation possible. They knew America was their new home, so they had to learn the language, and learn it fast.*

Others report regret over losing the ability to speak their mother tongue in a multicultural society where one language dominates.

> *Mercy: I struggle with keeping my Spanish. I do not really practice it as much as I would like. I do know it is important to me, so I make an effort to keep it fresh in my mind.*

*Alice: All of that [Spanish] on my side pretty much died out when my grandparents passed away.*

Some narrators act as ambassadors of language helping others who may be struggling with English or the mother tongue by serving as translators and interpreters in their respective communities. Many see themselves as providing a community service and usually they feel good about themselves afterwards. It is also a way to stay connected to the mother tongue. Here a narrator gives evidence of this:

*Nina: In the last 15 years, I thought that I had lost my Spanish since I really don't use it as much. But then I took a great journey to Cuba and it all came back to me, instantly. I became the United Nations for my traveling partners translating on our trip because none of them spoke Spanish. That was exhausting, but I learned, it never goes away. I thought I had lost it because I don't practice daily, but it came right back when I was back in a Spanish speaking country.*

The act of helping others who struggle with English extends far beyond the walls of work. Here is an example of a young narrator who regularly acts as an interpreter and translator in his private life:

*Israel: I help my mother all of the time when she's confused or shy about speaking to somebody in English I step in. When it comes to Spanish maybe a couple is in a restaurant or grocery store and somebody's speaking English to them and they don't know what's going on so again I step in and say something. It feels good whenever I help someone. I think I do it because I understand how it is going somewhere and not having a clue as to what's going on with the language. It can be difficult. I've seen my mother go through it and I feel if I'm in a position to help so, why not?*

*Section 3- Black English as Mother Tongue: Black in the Day* contains interviews with African-Americans on their perspectives on African American Language or what is commonly referred to as Black English, or Ebonics. "The fact is that most African Americans *do* talk differently from whites and Americans of other ethnic groups, or at least most of us can when we want to. And the fact is that most Americans, black and white, know this to be true" (Rickford & Rickford, p. 4).

I have included African Americans in this project because as speakers of Black English and American English I take the position that African Americans are bilingual and should be afforded the same resources as other ESL speakers such as those who speak Mandarin or Spanish. Beginning with the enslavement of Africans in colonial days Black English was born. It is a language based in English which has been Africanized by substituting English words with African ones:

> African American Language is a product of free African slave labor, having evolved from a 17th century Pidgin English that was a lingua franca in the linguistically diverse enslavement communities throughout Britain's North America colonies that became the United States of America. The pidgin blended European American English . . . with patterns from West African languages (see, e.g., Asante, 1990; Turner, 1949). The result of this blend was a communication system that functioned as both a resistance language and a linguistic bond of cultural and racial solidarity for those born under the lash. (Smitherman, 2000 p. 271-272)

Humans are born into a language and not only are we born into it but it is the embodiment of who we are as close to us as our DNA. Here narrators were asked: what do you consider your mother tongue to be and why? This is what they said:

> *Lorraine:* I consider Black English/Geechee my mother tongue. It is the language I was born into . . .
> *Crescent:* We speak what we call Slang. I really like it and my family brought me up on it . . . It's a part of being me.
> *Elnora:* I accept the notion that there is a language called Black English . . . I was born in Mississippi and so my parents and grandparents were raised as sharecroppers.
> *James:* It is the language of my youth. It's part of our private history—Black English—or more like a family heirloom handed down from generation to generation.

African-Americans have been forced to be bilingual as a result of living between two culturally different linguistic realities:

> *Kamaria:* The experiences I've had speaking mother tongue [Black English] in America has taught me that I had to learn how to communicate with different groups of people. I absolutely sound different depending on what the group is. For example, I attended a predominately white college and university so when I would respond to questions and participate in class discussions I knew that I had to speak in standard [American] English instead of expressing myself as I would with friends and family. I learned later in my life that this is called code switching, so I have learned how to be fluent in code switching where I will make it a point to say that, this, and there instead of dis, dat or dere . . .

I first heard the term Black English while I was a student enrolled in a socio-linguistics class at Fordham University. I became most interested in the scholarship of Dr. Geneva Smitherman and was introduced to her book, *Talkin and Testifyin*. In this groundbreaking work, "Dr. Smitherman makes definitively clear that Black English is a vital and effective language, as legitimate a form of speech as British, American, or Australian English" (inside front cover) Today, "the Black Idiom is used by 80 to 90 percent of American blacks, at least some of the time." (Smitherman, 1977, p. 2)

This stigmatized language, thought of as being spoken by the uneducated and consequently, the less intelligent is often made fun of in the media. Ironically, it is the lingua franca in popular American culture where for entertainment purposes its ubiquitous nature permeates television, movies and music:

> *James: In the late 80's while in college, I met a white fellow student who had never had a conversation with a Black person. Being very sincere, he complimented me on how well I spoke English and asked me who was my white example. Shocked, I told him that it was my parents who had taught me how to speak English. He said he thought that all Blacks spoke like the Blacks he'd heard on television. I guess he couldn't understand why I wasn't walking around saying "DYNOMITE" like the character JJ on the show Good Times.*

There is a tendency to dismiss Black English as slang. This is a "linguistic fallacy" according to Smitherman:

> The concept of "slang" does not begin to cover the broad range of semantic referents in the Black English vocabulary ... Slang suggests a highly specialized vocabulary used only by a certain group of people; the popular stereotype is that of teenagers, hustlers, hippies, musicians, and various and sundry characters of ill repute. Yet in the black community, the vocabulary of soul crosses generational and class lines and is grounded in black people's linguistic and cultural history. There are four traditions that Black Semantics draws from: West African language background; servitude and oppression; music and "cool talk"; and the traditional black church (Smitherman, 1977, p. 43).

It was unanimous among narrators interviewed for Section 3 that the workplace serves as a constant conduit for speaking American English and that if you do ever speak Black English at work you do so cautiously:

> *Crescent: If you spoke Slang [Black English] in the workplace it's likely that you would not get the job or let me say this you wouldn't be accepted by the other cultures because they would be afraid of you. You know the stereotype that if you speak Slang [Black English] then you're ghetto. You're uneducated. So, it's better to just speak proper [American English] in these situations.*
>
> *Elnora: So growing up I got through high school and went into the world of work. I ended up in occupations that required me to be in leadership roles. So this under pinned my way of speaking.*
>
> *Lorraine: It's okay to speak Black English in social settings with family and friends. I would say it is not okay to speak Black English in a professional business environment where people are conversing in Standard American English. I have often been in both professional and social situations where*

*another Black person and I spoke both. It was a cultural means of connecting and a symbol of unity and family.*

In *Tongue Shakers,* spoken language, a subject that binds us all, takes on different meanings as we strive to communicate organically with each other in our multicultural society. The fast pace of city life drives us away from one another and yet it brings us closer together. We must remain mindful of the fact that in America we encounter people from many cultures and that each culture is a unique expression of humanity deserving of the same respect we give to our own individual cultures. It is the freelance Ukrainian healthcare professional who works as a translator between doctors and patients. It is the Ethiopian business executive mom who speaks and writes fluent English at her job but who works just as hard keeping her mother tongue alive in her home so that her American born children can communicate with relatives living in Ethiopia. It is the little Chinese boy who struggles to learn English so that he can finally make friends with other children in his new American public school. It is the African American who must carefully pick and choose when it is best to speak Black English. It is the Hispanic family who retains their mother tongue while being just as fluent in English. As you read *Tongue Shakers* I ask you to think about your neighbor next door or the person you see every morning on your coffee run. This is their story on speaking mother tongue in our multicultural society—the story of ordinary people just like me.

# Section 1
# Mother Tongue Coming to America

*Tongue Shaker/ `tən –shāk- ər / n:* 1. one who defeats utterly a system of symbols for communication, esp. words used to represent assigned meanings and end as an effective force 2. one who creates a new vocabulary of a language, e.g., African-American Language, French Creole, Spanglish, Kombuis Afrikaans, Patois 3. one who cuts past the surface of the dominant language, often tossing it aside 4. one who uses the power of the spoken word to speak up and speak against oppression, suppression of religious views, and violations of civil and human rights 5. one who uses speech to effect political and social change 6. one who tells it like it is

### LIVING THROUGH THE BOSNIAN WAR

*Kristina K., age 25, Female*
*Birthplace - Zenica, Bosnia*
*Occupation–Bank Teller*
*Mother Tongue: Croatian*
*Speaks: American English*

It felt as if the whole world was being blown up. In the early 1990s my family and I —my mom, dad, and two brothers—were living through the bloody communal violence of a brutal war between the Serbs who as Orthodox Christians believe that Christ is a seed of life and forever remains the same (faith not based in science and philosophy), the Croats, who as Roman Catholics, believe that Christ is a seed of life that has grown into a tree (or believing in science and philosophy), and the Albanians who are Muslim and believe that the Prophet Muhammad is the messenger of God. It is said that the Bosnian War, with its ethnic cleansing campaign, is the deadliest European conflict since World War II and it is estimated that over 200,000 people died as a result of this war.

The thunder and lightning of bombs and guns, and the harrowing squeal of sirens crashed down above our heads, hitting the ground like blocks of heavy lead as we hid in the basement beneath a basement in cottages built to house thirty families. The cottages had no lights, no windows, and no running water. Each family hauled into the hole as many clothes and as much food as they could carry. Weighted down by fear, we huddled like rats. Whenever the bombs and guns grew silent we took turns climbing out of the hole to use the bathroom. This is also the time when men from certain families would sneak out to scavenge for any essentials left behind in the war's path. Nothing went unused. On one such mission, my father decided he and my oldest brother would sneak back to our house to gather more clothes. When they got to our home they found it had been blown up. Everything we owned in the world was gone. Literally, we were left with just the clothes on our narrowing backs.

Joining the 2.2 million people displaced by the war my father thought the only way for us to escape its ravaging grip was to migrate to Germany where we lived as illegal immigrants for six years. In the mid '90s the German government cracked down on illegals, particularly Croats who were told specifically to leave the country immediately or face deportation even though most of our homes were in Serbian controlled areas. Once again, we found ourselves in the position of having to pick up, leave, and start life all over again in a foreign land. My father, who had been fighting in the army on the American side thought it was best we go to America. I'll never forget the first day we arrived because we were each given a shot in the arm, and quarantined like lepers. I remember the shot so vividly because upon injection, it burned my entire body. I still have its searing scar on my arm.

Today, I am fluent in English but I found it difficult to learn. I took my first ESL class in the 3$^{rd}$ grade at an American public school, and it took another three years of taking classes before I started feeling comfortable speaking and writing the language. I learned English best by watching American TV. When I was a small girl my favorite shows for learning English were *Three's Company* and *Jerry Springer*. America is home to the largest overseas community of Croats in the world. My mother is a house wife who speaks absolutely no English, and my father, a welder, works at a company owned by a Croatian and he speaks very little English. My parent's neighborhood is a miniature Croatia, nestled and tucked away in the folds of America. There they have food markets, barbershops and hairdressers, novelty shops, restaurants, and an elegant hall used to host Croatian weddings and parties. Our Croatian-speaking Roman-Catholic church is located downtown.

My parents are old-fashioned and difficult, and they rarely find reasons to venture out of their neighborhood. There have been times when my mother and I were shopping outside of her neighborhood and I've seen people scoff and react to her as if she is being rude when she does not respond to them after they have spoken English to her. Sensing the dynamics of what's happening I come to her aid explaining to the person in my best English that my mom does not understand what they're saying to her because she doesn't speak English. Most people calm down after hearing this explanation but there are others who are insensitive, and act indifferent towards her as they toss quizzical glances her way.

I'm the opposite. I see America as an abundant vast country of opportunities and possibilities for its citizens to explore and experience. For me, the Croatian Diaspora extends way beyond the slim margins of my parent's tiny enclave. Instead, I live far away from my parents in a neighborhood where I work and live among people of different races and cultures. It does not please my parents to know that I have friends who are not Croatian. My boyfriend is African-American. I hold him close to my heart as a highly guarded secret. (Laughs)

Once, while over at my parents' visiting, I was talking on my cell phone to one of my American friends. My mother interrupted our conversation to ask me a question about dinner. Naturally, I responded back to her in Croatian. We talked back and forth for a few seconds. When we'd finished talking my friend who had been listening on the other end of the telephone asked me what were my mother and I talking about. I told her we were discussing dinner. My mother was preparing *pita*, a Croatian dish consisting of baked dough stuffed with spinach, topped with warm milk, butter, and egg. My friend laughed because she said our language sounded to her as if we were praying with each other. Surprised to hear this I laughed and assured her we weren't praying and translated to her in English what we had said in Croatian, although my friend and I both agree we can always use a prayer.

## ESL CLASSES BRINGS FRIENDSHIP TO A LITTLE BOY

*Chen H., age 34, Male*
*Birthplace–Taipei, Taiwan*
*Occupation–Student/Teaching Assistant*
*Mother Tongue: Mandarin*
*Speaks: American English, Japanese and French phrases*

China has twenty to thirty minority groups who speak different dialects of Chinese. Mandarin is the English of Chinese in that it is the standard version that is most spoken by speakers of Chinese. I have been in the United States since I was six years old. My parents didn't tell me much about us coming here other than we were taking a long trip. My parents entered a lottery of about 30,000 people who made application to come to the United States. There is usually a 10-15 year wait. My parents got lucky and won the lottery after only six months. This surprised my parents because they thought I would be in high school before we would be selected to come to the United States.

When I arrived in the United States I was confused because coming from a homogeneous society I grew up thinking that the whole world looked like me. We moved to Lexington, Massachusetts, in an all white community. I found going to school to be very hard because I couldn't speak the language and therefore I could not play with the other kids. My classmates acted as if they were afraid of me. I felt isolated. To compound things I started school at a time where ESL programs were not really established in many of the public schools. My cousin teases that I am the one who started the ESL classes in my neighborhood public school. It was my ESL teachers who kept me going and lifted my spirits during this difficult time. My regular teachers treated me as if I were retarded. Once the ESL program was officially established in my school I had friends to play with. My two best friends were from Hungary and Korea. We spent time playing a kind of game where we identified objects calling it by its correct name in English. We were learning words together and not so much complete sentences.

It was hard to apply my English lessons at home because at the time neither of my parents spoke English. Today, they both speak English fluently. My father also speaks Japanese and Spanish pretty well too because of his work on a large cargo fishing boat, which puts him in regular contact with people from Japan and Latin America. He majored in naval studies in high school where he learned to use a compass and read sea charts. This is before GPS so it was easy to get lost. When Taiwan was just beginning to industrialize, for double income, my father farmed during the day and fished in the evening.

I don't speak Mandarin much and find it more natural to speak English. Sometimes, I dream in Japanese. I'm single with no kids but if and when I do have children I intend to teach them Mandarin because it is part of their ancestry. I don't like that my parents never taught me Taiwanese. When I asked why, they said they didn't see a need for me to use it. I feel left out when I find myself in the company of Taiwanese speakers. I wouldn't want my children to feel this way. I know German and Danish students who speak five languages at one time. I believe knowing more than one language opens your eyes. You're able to touch more aspects of life. With every person I meet I learn something new.

The United States is globalizing at a rapid rate. There is a shift from the domestic student to the international student. Education is limited in certain parts of the world and the United States has a good educational system. Japan has an excellent education system so you won't find the Japanese immigrating to the United States to go to school. But, you will find that immigrants who come to the United States seeking a good education are mainly from Latin America, Turkey and other parts of Southeastern Europe, and Southeast Asia. I don't live in an Asian neighborhood. I'm American.

## AFRICA AT THE CENTER

*Amadou D., age 54, Male*
*Birthplace–Dakar, Senegal*
*Occupation–Merchant Entrepreneur*
*Mother Tongue: Fulani*
*Speaks: Wolof, French, American English*

I believe parents have to push their children to speak their native language. While growing up in Africa it was my mother who taught us to speak Fulani, our tribal tongue. I have faith that by teaching my culture to my children it will help them to build self-esteem. I teach my children that history and human civilization began with them—in Africa, and this is reason to be proud. History is distorted by whites and it is not taught properly in the schools. It is up to me to teach my children about Africa and the histories of other marginalized groups so that they can have a balanced perspective of the world.

In our family we take our American born children to Africa once a year during summer vacation months. We are careful not to treat them as tourists. Instead, we place each child in the home of African relatives where they wholly participate in the daily activities surrounding the family, like household chores and yard work, attending worship services at the masjid, and eating meals together. Making my children a part of my African family connects them to our African culture and history.

I speak four languages fluently: Fulani (my tribal language), Wolof (the official language of Senegal), French (Senegal's national language), and English. I even studied Russian in high school but rarely did I have the opportunity to speak it so it never developed. As a merchant, I trade African works of art and museum quality artifacts. My business puts me into contact with people who speak many languages but I find most everyone speaks English as well. Being multilingual has its funny moments. Sometimes when I'm trying to communicate in English my thinking is in French where words don't always correspond. I get the opportunity to speak Wolof often when trading in New York City because of its high Senegalese population. However, I believe it is rude for me or others to speak Wolof in the company of English only speakers.

## BRAIDING A PATH TO ENTREPRENEURSHIP

*Mary F., age 35, Female*
*Birthplace–Abidjan, Ivory Coast*
*Occupation–Salon Owner/Entrepreneur*
*Mother Tongue: French*
*Speaks: American English*

Learning to braid hair for us is a rite of passage. Just as girls in America are taught to cook, our mothers teach us at an early age to braid hair. I am a member of eBraiding, an online source for hair braiding in the United States. They have a group called *Women in Power* which helps African women to open salons in America. The group trains us to work in shops and it teaches us how to work with American customers. I have owned my salon for eight years.

At the age of twenty, I moved to America to work as a professional dancer with an African dance troupe. I lived in Poughkeepsie, New York, for a while as we toured cities along the East coast. I liked getting paid to dance. And, I was particularly struck by the freedom Americans have to go to school and to get work. I'm proud to be an African. God is the only one who knows why he made you.

French is my first language and English is my second language. Because I have no shame concerning my background, I am not afraid to speak French in the presence of English speaking Americans. There is pressure from this society to speak English only. For instance, I may be in my salon talking to one of my workers. Since she and I speak French, and what I am talking about to her does not concern anyone else present, I do not hesitate to speak French with her—freely and openly. It is our first language and we are comfortable using it. Americans present witnessing these exchanges seem to think we might be talking about them. I can tell by the look on their faces they are offended. I don't care. They are wrong. My attitude is when I need to talk with you I will speak to you in English.

I have taught my three American born children French which they speak fluently. When I am in public with my children I speak to them exclusively in French. I believe everyone needs time to speak privately with their relatives and friends.

## FROM DOCTOR TO TRANSLATOR

*Cheryl P., age 48, Female*
*Birthplace–Rovno, Ukraine*
*Occupation–Medical Translator*
*Mother Tongue: Ukrainian*
*Speaks: Russian, American English*

After World War II the Russian government placed a limit on the number of people in a family permitted to leave at any one time to visit the United States. The idea was that if a person left relatives behind they were certain to return back to Russia so that they could reunite with family members. I defected to the United States and am now a permanent resident.

My first language is Ukrainian, and I speak and write Russian and English. Back in my country I was a research doctor trained in the field of molecular biology. In the United States I'm no longer a doctor but my scientific and medical backgrounds helps me to work as a freelance interpreter where a university hospital hires me to translate vital medical information exchanged between its English speaking doctors and patients who only speak Ukrainian and Russian. I take my job seriously and I must be accurate. I feel like I provide service to the community. It's like holding the lives of many people in my hands. One wrong word, one miscommunication can literally translate into disaster.

The English I learned in the Ukraine was not good enough for me to understand and speak American English comfortably. I immersed myself in American culture and language. I watched television and took ESL courses. My Ukrainian accent is heavy and thick. I am treated differently when my accent is heard. People stare and start talking to me very slowly like I don't know what they're saying.

## LEARNING ENGLISH IN EXILE

*Draupadi 'Kamala' P., age 33, Female*
*Birthplace–Daga Dzong, Bhutan*
*Occupation–Laborer/Service Industry*
*Mother Tongue: Nepali*
*Speaks: Nepali, Hindu and American English*

*Author's Note: After several missed appointments in a neighboring library due to bad weather Kamala invited me to do the interview at her home. To my surprise and joy she sat me down with her entire family for a delicious vegetarian lunch. She told me that all who are invited to her home during meal time sit with the family. I felt truly welcomed by Kamala and her family.*

Margie: I remember when we started the interview earlier you said that here in America you felt like a brand new baby. Can you explain that for me?

Kamala: Actually, I was a little child when we were exiled from my country Bhutan. We came to Nepal and we stayed for twenty years. It wasn't that much of a difference. We are Nepalese and we used to speak Nepali. America is totally different from Nepal and Bhutan. I feel like I was born here or as newborn because when a baby is born they don't know about the world. I have to learn everything about this country. I have to learn each and every thing. Even for the coins we used to say rupees. Different names for different things like penny. We know that it's money. The names of the things are different so we have to learn everything. That's why I feel like a new born baby here. I spent one year here [learning the language] now I feel like I'm crawling. (Laughter)

*Margie: Do you feel that Americans are intolerant of accents? What happens when you talk to people you come into contact with on an everyday basis?*

Kamala: Thanks for asking that. Actually, what happened to me was when I came here I went to the post office and what happened to me was there was a lady she was African-American I didn't get here tone and she was actually speaking to me. I didn't get her tone but I understand her now. I know English I have a bachelor's degree from my country in English. My tone is different. The way we learn to speak here is different…it's made hard to understand some people. But I am starting to understand.

*Margie: You said tone, so how you say something?*

Kamala: Yes. Sometimes I feel sad because I can't understand people. For example, the way people say things have different meanings. We cannot understand the people's feelings if we don't know the tone. Native Americans speak fast others speak a little slower. People from Spain and Russia speak differently and Indians. They have different tones in America. Which is the right tone? [Laughter]

*Margie: You said you were exiled from your country. Can you tell me a little about that?*

Kamala: Yes. It is very sad to say we were exiled from the country. Bhutan is a small country. It's an Asian country, lays somewhere between India and China. Nepal is a neighboring country. There in Bhutan is Buddhism and Hinduism. I listened to my parents [to get the story]. We were exiled from the country because the leader of the country he was a follower of Buddhism. He wants to make everyone follow one religion in his kingdom. He wanted us to follow Buddhists culture. According to my feelings he may be good he wants to make same national race, same national language, same culture he wants to make. Those who are following another culture another language don't like to change. People who follow Hinduism don't want to change culture so there was a mass protest of Hindus who refused the King's new rules. [These leaders were rounded up and tortured and as a consequence of their protest and resistance they were asked to leave. In 1990-1992 the Nepalese people and the Hindu people left the country for safety.]

## BACK TO AFRICA

*Henry O., age 35, Male*
*Birthplace–Lagos, Nigeria*
*Occupation–Industrial Engineer/Project Manager*
*Mother Tongue: Igbo*
*Speaks: Igbo, American English, very little Yoruba*

Modern Nigeria and most of the continent of Africa are orthodox Christian or Muslim although traditional religions still do exist. The difference between those who don't practice Christianity or Islam in the West is that they are seen as not believing in God. This concept does not exist in Africa where people often turn to African traditional religions to supplement their orthodox religious beliefs.

There are over 250 languages with each worshipping two or three different gods within each culture. There are people who openly practice an orthodox religion while in secret they simultaneously practice a traditional religion, sort of as a backup. This phenomenon of observing two religions at once is mostly practiced by the older people fifty and over. Younger people are more loyal and faithful to the orthodox religions. Africans will come from America to consult with a priest in an African village to fix a personal problem while they are on vacation. The reading or consultation is conducted in Igbo or some dialect of Igbo.

My wife and I have a son but it will be up to my wife to teach him Yoruba, which is her mother tongue because I hardly ever speak Igbo anymore. We have learned a lot in America. We know how to build careers and professions. I have a degree in business and engineering and my wife is pursuing her business degree. One day I'd like to take all that I have learned back to Africa where my skills are needed. There are a lot of people in Africa who do not have the same skills and this would be a way to transmit, make good use of my skills at home, and it is a way for me to give back.

## THERE'S NO PLACE LIKE HOME

*Jodi N., age 21, Female*
*Birthplace: Cape Town, South Africa*
*Occupation: Chef*
*Mother Tongue: Afrikaans*
*Speaks: English, Kombuis Afrikaans*

I graduated from college in Cape Town with a national diploma in hospitality, which includes culinary arts and restaurant management. It was difficult to find a good paying job in Cape Town so I decided to sign up with a recruitment agency so that I could try to find opportunities to work abroad as a chef.

In January 2015, just a few weeks after being at the agency I got a call from my recruiter asking me if I was willing to leave South Africa in the next five weeks to start a twelve month internship in the United States of America. This news excited me, I immediately said yes. I was so overwhelmed and nervous at the same time. Here I was barely 21, sorting out the necessary documentation and making preparation for my journey to the States—a long three day journey I might add.

Two weeks before my departure I received heartbreaking news. My father was diagnosed with breast cancer. A male with breast cancer is very rare. The news completely broke me, after all I am his princess and he means everything to me. My father wished for me however to leave and to go and make the most of my time in the States. It was the most difficult decision to have to make but this was something I have always wanted to do and opportunities like this do not come every day.

My internship took me to Florida, the Sunshine State, where I work as a chef at a beautiful resort in Fort Myers Beach with some amazing people from all walks of life. I could not be any happier to be here. This was probably the best decision I have ever made despite the circumstances I had to come through.

I have traveled to many places in the world. People from the Netherlands understand slightly what I am saying because Afrikaans is very similar to Dutch. Speaking my mother tongue in the States is very difficult though because there are not many South Africans here who speak Afrikaans. There are some South Africans where I work but we speak different languages. Bear in mind, South Africa has eleven official languages. I speak two of them. How amazing is that? I would like to learn the others one day. I do not really speak my mother tongue in the States, unless it is on the phone to people back home in South Africa.

I notice in the States people look at me and automatically think I am Spanish or Indian. Without even asking what language I speak they just start speaking to me in Spanish and think I should understand it. It is like judging a book by its cover. I get that a lot. People are always surprised when they hear I am from South Africa and they find it hard to believe that people from Africa actually travel to the States. It is really sad how people think Africa is so behind the rest of the world, when it is actually not like that—again it is like judging a book by its cover. I always tell people who have that type of mindset to google South Africa so they can get an idea of what it is really like.

It is weird seeing so many foreigners working in the States. One day I would love to meet someone here I can communicate with in my mother tongue because it feels like a part of me is missing. I always notice how happy and comfortable my colleagues are speaking to each other and it is because they speak the same language.

In South Africa we use a dialect of Afrikaans called *Kombuis Afrikaans* which means "kitchen Afrikaans." It is a mixture of English and Afrikaans and is spoken among the younger generation who do not really feel the need to speak Afrikaans fluently. Afrikaans can be very complicated to speak which is why it is not spoken fluently any more. Elderly people tend to speak Afrikaans in the correct manner.

In my workplace I help people out on a daily basis with English. There are many people who I work with who do not speak English fluently. This causes a huge barrier in communication because it is difficult to get messages across to someone who does not understand and speak the same language.

Afrikaans is the most popular language in Cape Town so I never really have to help anyone out. However, there are many people who speak Afrikaans but are not fluent in English, mostly the elderly. This could be because many years ago education in South Africa was not as good as it is now and the elderly generation grew up in Apartheid where Black communities were treated as inferiors.

Under Apartheid "White" communities spoke English and Afrikaans fluently; "Coloured" communities spoke Afrikaans, not fluently though, which is how *Kombuis Afrikaans* developed. Apartheid, a phase which was abolished in 1994 when South Africa became a democratic country under president Nelson Mandela is a system where each race was treated differently. "White" people could go to places "Black" people could not go. Basically "white" people were treated better than "Black" people. This was at a time where discrimination against a person's physical skin color was a factor. Today, in South Africa, politically we have two race groups—white (very light skinned) and black (darker complexion). However, socially, we have three race groups—white, black and colored (a mixture of black and white).

Growing up in a middle class community my mother tongue became my second language and English became my first language. I grew up with parents who are fluent in English and I learned the language from them and from going to English schools. English is spoken throughout the entire world. Unlike Spanish for example, not many people understand and speak it. I met someone in the States whose parents are in their late 60's and they cannot speak English which is not a big surprise because as I mentioned earlier many elderly people from Cape Town cannot speak English or their English is limited.

Speaking my mother tongue is important to me because it is a part of my heritage. I am very proud to be a South African and speaking my mother tongue is something I am proud of too. I can be anywhere in the world but the fact that I know my mother tongue is something no one can take away from me.

People who speak English well are always so much easier to communicate with. Although English is spoken throughout the world, it can be misinterpreted because of a person's accent. Your English can be 100% fluent but if your accent is difficult to understand it does make it difficult for another person to understand what you are saying.

I personally do not have an issue with people who do not speak English well. Education is not always good in some parts of the world and I understand that not everyone is fortunate enough to receive a quality education. Sometimes, I do get irritated when people do not understand English especially when things need to get done quickly and trying to make them understand can take a longer time. However, I do think it is important to speak English well when you are working with the public. For example, if you are a waitress honestly the worst thing you can do is try to communicate with someone while offering a service to them and they do not understand what you are saying or you don't understand them.

I am not in America to find love. I am here to give my career a boost. Most likely I will marry someone back home because I want to settle down in Cape Town. When I do have children I will definitely teach them my mother tongue. It is important for children to know where their parents come from. I will also teach my children English because it is a language that is recognized throughout the world. I want my children to travel the world and to be able to communicate with others wherever they go. Today, things like getting a job and going to the university requires English.

Off topic I must tell you: The questions I get asked in America are really astounding and quite funny. It just shows you what some people actually think about Africans. I have been asked, "Do you live in a hut?" "Do lions walk in the street?" "So, if you're from Africa why you don't have weave in your hair?" "Why aren't you so dark?" And my favorite one, "What tribe are you from?" I did not have responses to these silly questions. Seriously, many Americans seem to think they are so much better than everyone else. It's a sad but true reality. Don't get me wrong Americans are nice people but some of them aren't open to getting to know other cultures. They always think everywhere else in the world is less "cool" than America. I say if people would take some time to get away from social networking and spend a little more time using Google to find out things they don't know about this country and other amazing countries for that matter then they would not look silly by asking silly questions.

## SPEAKING ENGLISH AND DRIVING FAST

*John T., age 31, Male*
*Birthplace–Monchengladbach, Germany*

*Occupation–Student*
*Mother Tongue: German*
*Speaks: English*

My father is taking English classes right now because he likes to travel. I started learning English as age 13. My grades were bad and I struggled. I wasn't comfortable making mistakes so I didn't perform well. I experienced a breakthrough when I participated in a high school exchange program which placed me in Michigan. I spent a whole year living with an American family who spoke only English. I had to talk to them and they had to talk to me. I made a lot of progress there. Speaking English got easier every day.

I live in England now as a student where I'm studying for my PhD in Biology. It's been 13 years since my last visit to the States and I notice a lot more security not so much in Europe. When I call my parents I speak German to them over the telephone. I think my accent is a positive thing. When people hear it they always try to guess where I'm from. When they find out I'm from Germany they try to speak to me in German—greetings like *guten tag* (good day). Americans usually know about the Autobahn because it is famous for not having speed limits. People like to drive fast.

## THE AMERICAN MYTH: SEEING IS BELIEVING

*\*Moussa D., age 44, Male*
*Birthplace–Dakar, Senegal*
*Occupation–Store Clerk*
*Mother Tongue: Fulani*
*Speaks: Wolof, French, American English, Russian, Tagalog*

I have two boys and one girl all born in Senegal. My children speak Arabic, French, English, and Spanish. I studied English before I came to the United States in 2000. I didn't like it [in America] so I went back to Africa the first time I visited here. The way America is described to us is not the reality. We are taught you come to America to make a lot of money. It's a myth. It's not as easy to make money as we are told. I feel in America you can make your own way but it's hard.

Another Senegalese owns the African market I work in. Back home I earned a B.A. in Linguistics but my degree is no good here. I went to Manhattan Community College to study computer science because that is what everyone is asking. I decided to do this after my first visit to America. I had to prepare my family for the reality of living and working in America. I first thought that I would be able to study in the United States and come home every two months. The reality is that I have to spend money for an expensive plane ticket and not work while in Africa; and I must contribute to my family so in reality I see my family every two years. I send money home to them weekly. One of these days my family will be able to come to the US to be with me.

I came to New York City first but it was too expensive. I worked as a waiter in a casino for a while. I lived in Alaska for seven years and made good money but got tired of the cold and loneliness. I decided to try Memphis where I met the gentleman who owns the market where I work now. I've been here three months.

Jum'ah service at the masjid is [spoken] in Arabic which is translated in African languages. My accent initially distances people but when they get to know me they say they like it. The market is across the street from a mixed continental African and African-American community. At work I get to speak my language regularly because most of our customers are Africans. Otherwise, I speak English, even with other Africans who do not speak Fulani, Wolof, or French.

*Margie: This is the end of the interview. Before I turn the tape off is there anything else you would like to share on topic or off topic?*
\*Moussa: Yes. Americans think we are ignorant. They ask us silly questions. How many wives do you have? Do you see lions? This makes me laugh because Dakar is a big city. Memphis is much smaller and less cosmopolitan than Dakar. I think America is so big and vast it needs one language to stay united.

## MOTHER AND DAUGHTER INTERVIEW

*Judith B., age 75, Female (Mother)*
*Birthplace - Tela, Honduras*
*Occupation –Director of Senior Citizen's Program (Retired)*
*Mother Tongue: Spanish*
*Speaks: American English, Spanish*

*Evelyn M. B., Age: 52, Female (Daughter)*
*Birthplace: Montclair, NJ*
*Occupation - Artist/Entrepreneur*
*Mother Tongue: American English*
*Speaks: American English*

*Author's Note: I first met Judith and her daughter Evelyn at a literary event at the Newark Public Library's Main branch. I noticed Judith's accent and told her about my project. We agreed to meet for an interview a few days later at her home. Before the interview Judith invited me to have lunch with her where she had prepared a delicious vegetarian meal. She graciously* opened up her home to me. At one point she shared family photos with me and old news articles. I really felt welcomed. Towards the end of the interview Judith's daughter Evelyn who was in New Jersey visiting from California returned from her errand and so we asked her to participate in the interview.

*Margie: Can you tell me a little bit about your experience with speaking Spanish in our multicultural society?*
Judith: I was born and raised in Tela, Honduras, so my native tongue is Spanish. English as a language was not too hard for me to speak because my parents were from Belize [formerly British Honduras which is an English speaking country]. They sent me to Belize to go to school and study English [British]. When I came to America in 1958, I found it easier to adapt to my new English speaking surroundings because I was already speaking the language. On my first job I worked as a nanny taking care of two Jewish-American English speaking children so therefore, I only spoke English. However, at my next job as a nurse at Mountainside Hospital in Montclair, New Jersey, I began to use my Spanish socially because many of the staff members were Spanish. When I got my last job working with the City of Newark (29 years), it was the first time I used my native tongue—Spanish.

*Margie: As a part of your job?*
Judith: Yes.

*Margie: What exactly did you do? How were you able to use your Spanish?*
Judith: I helped with the Spanish clients who could not speak English. They always needed an interpreter. So I was an interpreter. Because I was bilingual I was someone they could relate to because I spoke the language. I communicated the needs of the Spanish speaking clients to my employer who in return became better equipped to service the client's needs.

*Margie: Now, were you officially an interpreter or is this something that was done informally?*
Judith: It was just something that was just given to me because there was not anyone else on staff who could speak Spanish.

*Margie: What type of services were you providing?*
Judith: Housing and social services. I was very helpful. If someone came in looking for housing or needed assistance in welfare I would be the one to redirect them or if they needed employment I was the one to direct them to those resources.

*Margie: What kind of Spanish speakers were they? Were there immigrants coming from the Portuguese section?*
Judith: The Spanish speakers were mostly Puerto Rican but some were Portuguese, Chileans and Dominicans. Their languages are basically the same but different tongues. With the Portuguese, you really have to think about what they're saying to try to get at what they mean.

*Margie: Do you think your accent distances people or brings them closer to you?*
Judith: I find that my accent brings me a little closer to some people.

*Margie: Ok. Can you tell me what you mean?*
Judith: When I'm talking to people they understand that I'm a foreigner and people pay more attention to me. That can be good and that can be bad because people have a tendency to treat foreign Blacks better than American Blacks. You know at the time I came to America there was a lot of prejudice against Blacks and with my black skin they never knew that I spoke another language...even to the Spanish people they think when they see me they see a Black [American] but as soon as I speak and they find out I'm Spanish I'm accepted. If a Spanish person is talking to another Spanish person I listen to see if they're talking about me before I turn around and say something in Spanish. (Laughs)

*Margie: Can you give me an example of that happening to you?*
Judith: Ok. For instance, one afternoon I was out shopping with my friends and it looked as if I tried to go forward in the line. This Spanish woman said to her friend in Spanish, "don't let that Negro person get in front of you!" I turned around and said in Spanish, *"no estoy tratando de ponerse en frente de usted* [No. I'm not trying to get in front of you]. Then she said in English, "Ai, you speak Spanish?" And, I said, *"Perfecto."* Everything changes once they find out that you speak Spanish. Attitudes change and they become nicer.

*Margie: I want to ask your daughter something. The fact that you don't speak Spanish do you feel left at all?*
Evelyn: Truthfully, I do speak some Spanish but I understand it more than I can speak it. I don't speak it as fluently as my mother. When I'm around my mother's family and friends and they are speaking Spanish they always translate their conversations in English so I can understand their point of views. Sometimes, though they don't have to interpret anything for me because I can comprehend and understand them completely. So no, I don't feel left out.

The only time I really do feel left out is when I am among Spanish speaking strangers who will purposefully speak Spanish in a negative tone to avoid making a connection with me. Since I know some Spanish and I'm familiar with derogatory Spanish words and phrases I can get the gist of the conversation. I believe this is due to the color of my skin which is black like my mother's.

I identify very strongly with my African roots because my father and mother spent time teaching me about my African/African American heritage. After my parents separated when I was around six years old my grandmother and aunt came from Honduras to live with us in America. So you see, I was a child raised well into my teen years in a bilingual, female dominated, Honduran/American household. Because of this I do feel a certain familial connection with Spanish speaking people not only through the language we share but through other aspects of the culture as well like the foods we eat, the music we listen and dance to, the folklore or family stories told to me by my grandmother and aunt, the mores and morals that my mother lives by, and my family's religious and spiritual practices. It was everyday life!

*Margie: Judith, what are the reasons why you didn't teach Spanish to your daughter? Was it a conscious decision?*

Judith: Because my husband was an [African] American I didn't speak much Spanish at home unless I called up my sister or my mother on the telephone. When she [her daughter] was growing up I wanted her to mainly concentrate on English because education is very important to me. Yes, education is very, very, very important. Even my cousins from back home when they came here I said it's good that you speak Spanish but you got to learn the other language too because it's important. I used it on my job and it was important when I worked.

Evelyn: It was my mother's choice not to teach me Spanish and I respect and understand that choice. However, it was hard for me not to pick up some Spanish from my family at home because I heard it all of the time. Also, I studied Spanish in high school for a year. In fact, when I was 14 years old I spent the summer with my aunt and her family in Honduras. I learned to speak Spanish fluently but I lost it in a few months after returning to America because my social environment did not support my Spanish. As the saying goes, if you don't use it you tend to lose it!

*Margie: Now Judith, I want to ask you one more thing before I end the interview. What opportunities do you have to speak Spanish now that you are retired?*

Judith: Spanish has become more incorporated into American culture. I have the opportunity to speak Spanish every day. For example, at the marketplaces, the bodegas, and other business I frequently patronize are owned by Spanish speaking people. I watch the Spanish Novellas on Spanish television daily. Most of my family, friends, acquaintances and neighbors speak Spanish so it's not likely I'll forget the language. [Laughs] Speaking Spanish is as important to me as is speaking English.

*Margie: Well, I'm going to end the interview right here. Do you have any last things you would like to say before we end the interview Judith?*

Judith: Yes. I am hoping with the interview we did today along with my daughter I hope more people would be able to communicate with Spanish people in both languages and more people should learn another language so that they are able to relate to other people.

## I CAN'T TALK TO MY GRANDMOTHER

*\*Irene C., age 31, Female*
*Birthplace –Brunei (Island near Malaysia)*
*Occupation –Art Director*
*Mother Tongue: English*
*Speaks: English*

*Author's note: I met \*Irene and her friend at Graceland while they were vacationing from Australia.*

My parents met in London. My dad is originally from Brunei and my mother is from Malaysia. They married and my dad brought us back to Brunei which is where I was born. They speak different dialects so that's why they decided to raise my brother and me speaking English only.

However, it's kind of annoying because then we moved to Australia so I never really got to learn how to speak Malay or one of the dialects they speak in Brunei and so I can't speak to my grandmother who lives in Brunei and speaks no English. She can kind of understand English and I can kind of understand Malay so we can kind of communicate, but not really.

While I was growing up we'd visit Brunei about every two years at Christmas time. It's been 13 years since my last visit. My father has nine siblings so I have a lot of cousins who would translate while I talked to my grandmother. It's just not the same and I regretted then and now not being able to communicate with her because my cousins told me that my grandmother tells great stories. You want to be able to just talk to your grandmother and not have to wait for someone to translate.

I've always wanted to come to America so my friend and I are visiting from Australia. We started in Los Angeles where we bought an old car. We're driving across country for the next six months. We both really love music and it a big part of our tour. We're making our way through the south, up to New York, across the north then back to the west coast.

Growing up in Australia I'd often be mistaken for someone who doesn't speak English. I might go to a supermarket and the cashier starts talking to me very slowly or I get people who approach me for help because they think that I speak Mandarin or some other Asian language.

## ETHIOPIAN AT HEART

*Yonas Tesfaalem A., Age 31. Male*
*Occupation: Gas Station Clerk*
*Birthplace: Addis Ababa, Ethiopia*
*Mother Tongue: Amharic*
*Speaks: Tigera, American English*

My mother and father were born into farmer families. When my mother was seventeen she moved to Addis Ababa where she worked in a restaurant as a washer. At age twenty-two my father became a carpenter then he improved himself and got a license to own a truck and drove it in Ethiopia for over forty years. My father has four wives and seventeen children.

Here is where my story gets complicated. The country next to us, Eritrea, used to be a part of Ethiopia but in 1991 it received independence through war. After that we got peace and everything was nice. No war. No nothing. Then in 1998 the Eritrean-Ethiopian war broke out and Eritrea started kicking everyone out who was not Ethiopian and Ethiopia started kicking out everyone who was Eritrean. Since my dad was born in Eritrea and I lived in Ethiopia I couldn't get ID or stuff like that. If the government found out you had Eritrean blood they would come to your house at say, 5:00 in the morning when no one can see. They wake you up and take you to the bottom and drop you off without your stuff just with whatever you are wearing. So things you worked for twenty or thirty years they would take them from you and you lost everything. My mom died so since my dad is Eritrean I was kicked out of Ethiopia which is why I left to join my auntie in America.

I first went to Nairobi, Kenya, where I stayed for one year then I came to Atlanta where I started high school in the 11$^{th}$ year. I started working at Subway and going to school at the same time helping my own self since I was a teen-ager. I finished high school in an open campus school. That's where people over eighteen can go there to finish. I just applied for U.S. citizenship this year.

In America I have mixed friends. Sometimes things happen, you know minor stuff that I don't pay much attention to. People be like, "What language you talkin'?" I tell them, "Amharic." Then they say, "Amharic oh, ok." Most people don't even know. That surprises me. I have maybe fifteen friends here who I can speak Amharic with.

At first it was hard learning to speak English but after a year it got easier after I started reading ESL language books because they're easier to read. I use to write the English words on a piece of paper. I had my country's dictionary so I would write on top of the paper the meaning in my language. When I went somewhere and wanted to start talking to somebody I read the stuff off of the paper and I would say, "Hey, where are you from?" That's how I used to talk to people here. After people started responding to me my confidence level went up and I said to myself, Ah ha, they understand me I'm doing good. So that's how I learned English.

Speaking my mother tongue is important to me because that's the first language I opened my mouth with. Nothing would cause me to lose it because I came here when I was older. You don't forget your culture and sometimes you get more friends from back home who don't speak English so it's good to speak the language. I like people who speak English well. It makes me want to talk like them—I want to speak it perfect like water flowing over.

People who don't speak English well I want to help them more. Even if I don't speak their language I know they want something they just don't know how to say it. I try to understand their body language and whatever stuff they are pointing to. I don't get mad with them. I go one by one until we figure it out. I'm patient with people who speak another language.

Maybe in the next three years I will save enough money to get my own license so that I can drive a truck like my father. I'll work for about a year and save some money then I'll get married. Of course, I will teach my children my language. It's good for them to have in case they go visit their father country they won't get confused and will be able to speak and they will be able to say hey, I speak two languages, I'm bilingual.

*Margie: Well, I'm going to end the interview now; is there anything you'd like to share with me on or off topic before I turn the tape off?*

Yonas: I want to share that I want people in America, my people, Black people to visit Africa so that they can see what's going on there. We should be connected instead of disconnected. They will love it. Why only white people travel to Africa? We would love to see our Black brothers and sisters too.

## THE ROAD TO ENGLISH IS LONG

*Heriberta R., Age 43, Female*
*Occupation: Homemaker*
*Birthplace: Toluca, Mexico*
*Mother Tongue: Spanish*
*Speaks: American English*

I was born in Toluca, Mexico. I lived with my father until I was 2 years old. My mother left my father because he whipped her. We moved to (inaudible). My mother left us to go to work. She gave money to my grandmother to help raise us. I married at 15 years old and came to Dallas, Texas with my husband. I stayed in Dallas for 10 years then I moved to Memphis. I have five children. Two girls and three boys.

Sometimes it's hard because some people don't try to understand us. I didn't have opportunities to go to school because I am home with my children. And some people are angry with that because they don't understand the Spanish.

I went to school for ESL but for only a couple of months. I try to learn English from my oldest son. All of my children speak Spanish and English. They translate for me sometimes and help me to sign the papers.

The church I go to is two communities—African-American and Spanish. Sometimes I help Spanish people in church who don't understand the English part of the service. I don't want to lose my language tongue because it is important to know two languages—to be bilingual. It's more opportunities for jobs. My daughter gets paid more money on her job because she is bilingual.

*Margie: What is your attitude towards people who speak English well?*

Heriberta: I feel good about them. I wish I could learn more English like them. It's important because I live in the United States. I know English is the language of this country. That's why I try to learn more English because it's a part of this country.

*Margie: I'm going to end the interview right now. Is there anything on topic or off topic you would like to say?*

Heriberta: Well, there is discrimination in the work and sometimes it's hard. Not for me but for my husband who works for his self. Sometimes he don't get work because he's Spanish.

## LEARNING BY WATCHING

*Amatoulaye B., Age 25, Female*
*Occupation: Hair Stylist*
*Birthplace: Conakry, Guinea*
*Mother Tongue: Fulani*
*Speaks: French, Arabic, Sou Sou, Maninke, American English*

*Margie: Tell me a little bit about your family background.*

Amatoulaye: We're from Conakry, Guinea, and we came there when I was twelve years old. My father was here [America], first he left the family and came here in 1995. He started working and providing for the family. He sent for my mother and brothers and sisters. So when I came here first we lived in New York. I had to learn to speak the language. I didn't know nothing [reflects] how to say hi or bye or even how to say open the door.

*Margie: How did you learn the language?*
Amatoulaye: When we came to Memphis I was in the fifth grade so I was already going to school back in Africa but I was going for French, so I studied French from kindergarten to fifth so when I got here I had to switch over from French to English so I had to learn my ABC's and 1,2,3's at the age of 12. I also took ESL classes. It was kind of a weird feeling because the language I was hearing didn't sound like a language to me so I had to really catch on to what people were saying. The way we sound when we speak Fulani or Sou Sou sounds gibberish. This didn't sound like that. How I learned to speak English was through the actions. I had to learn it by watching people's actions when they talked. How they moved their hands and their face in order for me to learn it.

*Margie: Can you tell me about your experiences speaking Fulani in our multicultural society?*
Amatoulaye: When I start speaking Fulani the instinct is to mix it up with English. I speak Fulani at home with our family but sometimes we make a mistake and speak it with a regular American. Sometimes we forget to speak certain words in English. We have to stop and think about it. We know how to say it in Fulani but we don't know how to say it in English. It's like you're juggling two languages. Our language we speak it fluently there is nothing we don't know how to say.

*Margie: Have there been times when you've had to help someone with language maybe in your community?*
Amatoulaye: There were times when my uncles and aunties who come from the same part of Africa where I'm from and they speak no English or French. They only speak Fulani, Sou Sou or Maninke. Some of the older ones never went to school, they didn't have the opportunity over there so we strive to provide because we have the mentality that God gave everybody knowledge so we believe in that. So they don't even know how to write the letter "a" they may know how to write some Arabic so I have to fill out applications for them and do letters for them help them spell out their name. Even my own mother I had to teach her how to write and help her and now she knows how to write [English] and she never went to school a day in her life.

*Margie: Is speaking English important if you live and work in America? Why or why not?*

Amatoulaye: Yes. It's important because the English language is number one in the world, it's a popular language. If you speak English you can communicate with many people in the United States. Many people with different races and different cultures and in order for us to communicate we have to speak English.

*Margie: Why is speaking your mother tongue important to you?*
Amatoulaye: Because I think it is so powerful and it's good where you can grow up speaking your language without having to go to school for it. I have little sisters and brothers and I have seen other African kids here who grew up here and were born here and they speak their [African] language. They speak their tongue language and they have never been to Africa a day in their life.

*Margie: What is your attitude towards people who speak English well?*
Amatoulaye: The attitude I have is that some of them when you're not an English speaking person you speak it with limits and people have to understand this. There is going to be a part of the language that you're not going to understand unless you learn it again. A language goes deep where the people who speak it are still learning it. I try to think of my language. When I want to talk I talk in my language in my head and respond in English. [Laughs] I do that, I have to visualize the words.

*Margie: What is your attitude towards people who do not speak English well?*
Amatoulaye: I like to teach them. I will be very happy to meet them and I like to help them out. I would hope that I speak it well so that they understand.

*Margie: What could cause you to lose your mother tongue?*
Amatoulaye: Yes. I have seen some people lose it. I have been in the United States for 12 years so in order for me to lose my mother tongue I would have to not be around my people. Say if I moved off by myself and would be around just Americans where I would speak English more it would break down my language. Or every time I speak my language I would mix it with English until it's gone. I don't believe I'll ever lose my mother tongue because I was born in Africa. Now, Africans born in the United States or London lose their mother tongue all of the time.

*Margie: Does your child who was born in America know your mother tongue?*
Amatoulaye: I have one son seven years old and he speaks Fulani. His father is African-American so when he goes to his father's family they all

speak English and when he's with my family we speak Fulani so he speaks both.

*Margie: I'm going to end the interview now but before I turn the tape off is there anything you'd like to add on topic or off?*
Amatoulaye: Yes. I'd like to say that I enjoyed myself talking to you in the interview. It makes me feel good because it feels like I went back to Africa for a second. [Laughs] Having the chance to talk about my country and to have someone from here who is interested in my culture makes me feel good. It makes me feel like we're connecting to each other to the point where one day we'll look up and all of us will speak the same language.

## FOREVER MOTHER TONGUE

*Juan C., Age 48, Male*
*Occupation: Unknown*
*Birthplace: Quito, Ecuador*
*Mother Tongue: Spanish*
*Speaks: English, French*

*Author's note: I met Juan and his family while they were vacationing at Graceland. Juan and his family reside in Honduras.*
I grew up in Ecuador where I went to school in the city of Quito. I have three brothers and one sister. I came to San Francisco to finish my high school and university studies. I did this with my own money. I have two master's degrees; one in sociology and the other in political science. My father is an engineer and my mother is a homemaker.

In Europe it's not a big issue speaking another language because there you have many languages. However, in the States it is difficult because most of the people speak only one language and they get mindful of you and scared when they start hearing you speak another language. I don't know why people here are like that. They believe everybody should speak English and that's not the case. I like Europe much better where you can speak different languages all of the time and it's no problem. But here, yes, it's a big problem.

Most of the time people here relate to the accent. They believe the accent that everybody should have is the American accent and unfortunately it is not. There are many accents for the English language and people have to get used to that. Not everything and everybody sounds the same. People should learn to speak slowly—that's the problem when they don't speak slowly they don't articulate. They speak fast because they think everyone should understand whatever they say and that is not the case. Sometimes, it's much, much more difficult and the people here are not just friendly that way.

I have three daughters and all of them are bilingual as well as my wife. The more languages you know the better it is for my children and me because in this world you need to know more than one language. For me, it's not just related to culture but to knowledge.

*Shaheed: I'm going to end the interview now. Is there anything on topic or off topic you would like to say?*
Juan: Yes. For me I think that the American people should learn more languages and they should give more value to the people who are bilingual or trilingual because there are many of us here. Most of the time when people arrive here they want to forget their mother tongue because they want to be integrated. Integration is not a reason to lose your mother tongue.

## AMERICANS HELP ME SPEAK ENGLISH

*Ilias B., Age 34, Female*
*Occupation: Housewife*
*Birthplace: Conakry, Guinea*
*Mother Tongue: Fulani*
*Speaks: French, Sou Sou, Mandingo, American English*

I've been in United States for twelve years. My mom and father were born in Guinea. My sister raised me in Conakry since I was two years old until I got married. She treated me nice and was very kind to me. Me and my mom are not that much in touch at the time I was growing up but we are in touch now. My father is dead.

In America I have met some Fulani people here so we can communicate because we came from the same country. It helps me not to feel alone in America. But Fulani is just for your people. Memphis is very big so you have to learn to communicate.

I used to work in a warehouse and I had friends who helped me and I took ESL but not that much. I started speaking English two years after I'm here. And the people I met when you ask them questions I really appreciate they answer you. Even though they know that I don't speak good English they try their best to help me and to try to make sure they know what I mean. Many that I have met do not laugh or they do not say bad things.

It's important for my family to speak Fulani that is what I know. I can understand when someone speaks to me in Fulani or try to explain something in Fulani. I feel happy you know because I can understand everything. I am very excited to come and listen because I can understand the whole word. With English sometimes I cannot understand the meaning cause it's in English. I got a book the Quran where they did the meaning in Fulani so I can read Fulani and I was very excited cause I said wow I can understand this better. When I read English I go to the dictionary [for] each word it makes me very tired you know. The mother tongue is very good.

My three children were born in the United States. They speak Fulani a little but I don't know what happened they speak mostly English. It's important because I don't have my family here so they just know strangers...it's hard for them to see my uncle's daughters because they live in another state and it's hard to meet together so when they learn Fulani it helps me to connect them with my family. Like when I call my mom in Africa my daughter say, "Mommy what is she trying to say to me?" I tell them they need to increase your speaking in Fulani.

*Margie: Are you learning English from your children?*
Ilias: Yes. Lately, since they speak it at home it helps me a lot.

*Margie: Do they translate English for you?*
Ilias: Yes my oldest daughter [11 years old] helps me a lot. If I don't know something she will explain it to me.

## TRANSLATING FOR LOVE

*\*Rose D., age 16, Female*
*Birthplace–Memphis, TN*
*Occupation–Student*
*Mother Tongue: Spanish*
*Speaks: American English*

I'm in the 9$^{th}$ grade. My mother was born in San Luis Potosi, Mexico, and my father was born in Puebla, Mexico. My mother tongue is a dialect of Spanish and an ancient Native American language. I was born in the United States but as a very young child I attended school in Mexico. We came back to the States when I was in the 3$^{rd}$ grade. I started learning English. My parents moved here to get better jobs and better schools for me. My father is fluent in English and works outside of the home. My mother is a stay at home mom who doesn't speak English—only a little bit. She's afraid to mess up. My grandmother on my mother's side lives with us and she speaks no English.

I started translating for my mom and grandmother two months after I began taking ESL classes in the 3$^{rd}$ grade. I liked learning a new language and new customs. I plan to take French in the 10$^{th}$ and 11$^{th}$ grades. I have two friends at school who speak Spanish. We talk to each other in a combination of English and Spanish—more Spanish if we want to say something in private. I like moving through the languages. I try to teach my mom English—she understands it better than she speaks it. If my mother has business to take care of she will pick me up from school early so that I can go with her to translate. This makes me feel important. I will teach my children both languages but Spanish first. I don't like to speak slang only proper English. But, I speak it sometimes to be cool. My favorite subjects are math, biology, and I'm an honors English student.

My parents say I'm too young to have a boyfriend but I kind of have one anyway at school. He's African-American. My mother told me that once I'm allowed to date that I can't bring home an African-American boy—only Mexican or white—or she'll kick me out of the house. I told her that if he likes me and I like him and if he's cute then I'll just have to leave home.

## FROM ROME WITH LOVE

*Anna S., Age 45, Female*
*Occupation: Social Worker*
*Birthplace: Rome, Italy*
*Mother Tongue: Czech/Italian*
*Speaks: American English*

I was born in Rome, Italy, while my mom was there visiting. Both of my parents are Czech my father resided in Prague the capital of the Czech Republic. It was Czechoslovakia at the time. After I was born we moved back to Prague where we lived for about a year. It was Communist at the time and so my mother escaped with a fake passport with my brother and me in tow. We lived in Rome for about 4 or 5 years then we moved to Chicago where we lived for a year and then we moved to Memphis where I have lived off and on ever since. My transition from Rome to Chicago was smooth. It helped that I knew a little English, that I was only 5 years old and resided around others who spoke English. I attended a school that was quite good. In fact, when we moved to Memphis I was actually a grade ahead.

Czech is not a popular or common language in the United States so mostly I just speak it at home with my mom. I understand it a lot better than I speak it. My mother talks to me in English too so I'm not as fluent as I would be if I lived in Prague. When I go visit my family overseas I do talk Czech with them. Again, my Czech is rusty but they take the time and correct me. My mom doesn't do this and I wish she would. I want to know what's right and what's wrong. I think it would really be cool for me to take a class in Czech language and learn it from the outlook of an academic because I'm spotty with a lot of verb conjugation and it's kind of a complicated language so that would be cool.

With Czech I never encounter anyone having problems with the language. I don't remember my Italian so I couldn't help anyone there. But with English of course as a therapist I work every day helping people with therapy and insurance. I do speak a little Spanish because for a short time I was married to a man from Argentina. We lived in south Florida. Sometimes I serve people who speak only Spanish so I'm able to speak to them in Spanish, poorly, but they seem to understand me.

Speaking my mother tongue is important to me because when I hear the language I melt on the inside because it's a kind of comforting and nurturing sound. This is probably because it reminds me of the time when I was living with my whole extended family, when we were all together in Prague. If you were to hear Czech it's not harsh sounding like German so when I think about Czech I think about the fairy tales or stories I read as a little girl. Czech for me represents my little girl self. Calling it my mother tongue makes me think of my mother immediately.

Czech is important in keeping connected to my family. It's expensive to fly there and I'm more of a person who likes to see people. I'm not really into texting and social networking. I don't get to go overseas as often as I would like to. I do have family on my dad's side who have invited me to spend time with them at their cottage in Prague. I would very much like to renew this alliance. If they were in the next state it would be different. Sometimes I get mad about my family being together and I can't be with them. I feel jealous because they get to do things together and I'm way over here.

My mom is 77 years old and she's not feeling well right now. Her passing would definitely diminish my exposure to Czech. The other day my mom expressed concern that I would not be able to communicate with my family properly if she dies. I became inwardly annoyed as I know I could give more effort to contacting them but I don't want to. However, if my mom died then I probably would reach out to them more to make up for her absence. Also, they have rarely visited us but that would be great if they did.

## SPEAKING FULANI, CONNECTING TO HERITAGE

*Madinah D., age 23, Female*
*Birthplace: Mauritania*
*Occupation: Recent college graduate*
*Mother Tongue: Fulani*
*Speaks: American English, Arabic, Urdu, Hindi, French*

My father was working in the United States and he applied for my mother and me to join him. We moved to Memphis, Tennessee in 2002. I love the fact that I can speak to my parents in Fulani and other family members in the United States. I particularly love meeting a Fulani from another city in America and communicate with them in our mother tongue. The language bonds us together. At home everyone speaks Fulani but speaking it here allows for more privacy.

I've been studying English since the 2nd grade. I help people in my community all of the time [with English]. I translate letters, help with job applications, give advice, and I go to the hospital with people many times. Being able to communicate in English gives me both independence and privacy because I read my own letters and I go to the hospital on my own.

Speaking Fulani is important to me because it reminds me of my heritage and serves as a connection to my people. I speak English primarily in my life. Just as Fulani connects me to my heritage and people, English connects me to America and Americans. This is not to say that I consider people who don't speak English any less American. I also appreciate the fact that, for the most part, the world speaks English.

I try to be very patient with people who don't speak English well. It's not their fault and they shouldn't be made to feel bad about not speaking it well. It doesn't make them dumb or uneducated. In my experience, they are usually people who were top students in their countries.

When I have children I will definitely teach them Fulani so that they can stay connected to their people. It is also a must that my children speak English so I will absolutely teach them that too.

## PATOIS FROM THE ISLAND OF JAMAICA

*Deta G., Age 64, Female*
*Occupation: Multi-media artist*
*Birthplace: St. Andrews, Jamaica*
*Mother Tongue: English/Jamaican Patois*
*Speaks: English*

I was born to Anna Delissa Palmer a single middle-aged woman of Jamaican ancestry and my father's name is Albert Nathaniel Salmon who was also Jamaican but they come from two different parishes. My mother's family lived in the parish of Manchester which is up into the Blue Mountains. My father lived on the other side of the mountain in a parish called Saint Elizabeth which is near the Savannahs and big rivers.

Given the history of the English and the various European cultures that dominated Jamaica, the slave inhabitants who were brought to Jamaica during the enslavement period and through multiple sets of waves of migrations lived in sub groups. People living in these isolated areas bred a variation of different languages and cultures. So, even though both my parents are Jamaican they share very different intra-cultural practices.

My father's family was thought to be part Taino so there are a lot of Native American practices that infuses his side of the family. He would be considered African and somewhat Amerindian. On my mother's side there was no direct evidence that she had any mixture of Amerindian or European cultures although it was rumored that she was Fante because some of the words she used and the little songs she would sing which were taught to her by my grandmother were Fante songs. It was somewhat confirmed that my maternal grandmother had a cousin in Ghana in the 1800's who was writing to people in Jamaica.

In terms of my experiences with speaking patois, I discovered in Jamaica that I spoke a very dense patois that was essentially African. The insinuations, the coloring and the way in which the language is verbalized and practiced would be closer to an African peoples' of West Africa. It was less sanitized than the patois that was spoken in the commercial areas of Kingston where tourism dominated. This caused concern for my mother. There was this idea that if you spoke patois that you were low class and not bright and it clearly opened you up to more discrimination and exclusion. Because my mother saw those things and she wanted to help prepare me for the new world she provided me with a private finishing education to try to soften the idiomatic and heavy brogue of the African patois I was used to speaking.

My mother started early doing things like not speaking the patois at home. She would only bring it out when we had cultural events. Those times when she really wanted to put on or to show people that we had something really deep going on outside of their reign. But on a daily basis my mother spoke a light lilting English that was meticulous and considered King George's English in an effort to help normalize my own English.

Patois is different from English in that because of the dominance of the African tribal influence then the idiom is an African one. In terms of behaviors when speaking the language, especially non-verbal communication and particular words are somewhat similar to the African American language, which evolved primarily as an attempt to resist the planter's influence and the slave master's knowledge of what people were doing or saying. So there was a concerted attempt to create a communication system that was out of the reach of the regular understanding of the dominant language. I would still say today patois is a language of political resistance and recovery of identity.

At the turn of the 19$^{th}$ century we had a large wave of Indians from India to come settle in Jamaica to sell soft textiles. They came with their languages and also they were inculcated with the prejudices of the white man. They literally walked into Jamaica and begin showing domination towards the native people who were essentially Negroid or Black. Many of the earlier resistances started coming back. Black people tried to create separation in terms of how they would gather, what they would do and how they would resist and fight in the local skirmishes arising from the conflict with immigrants who behaved like the slave master.

After coming to America the first thing people would say is to me is that I don't sound Jamaican. I would say, "how so? What does sounding Jamaican mean to you?" They would say, "oh, you don't use the funny language." And

I would say, "oh, but I do!" I'm aware that because I went to finishing school patois was discouraged in terms of your daily interactions with people so that you would be able to assimilate. Although you hide your patois you know it's your protection but you don't want people to first experience it so that they can discriminate against you. Of course I don't mind translating patois to non speakers but no matter how well I translate I get to maintain a part of the meaning for myself which is really comforting and unspeakable. It goes to the root of my African identity keeping me connected to what it means to be an African person no matter where I am. I think that's very helpful especially for people like myself who came to the West Indies because of slavery but who were lucky enough to retain a strong aspect of the culture which is language.

I become immediately relaxed when I speak patois. The language is so heavily insinuated with many hidden metaphors which allow me to say things on a deeper level. It's *a jokey fine* meaning a language that teases. Teasing in Jamaica is a cultural requirement. It breaks the ice. I would like to say that this whole issue of language is absolutely at the heart of each individual's identity. It is extremely sacred. It's not just African Americans who are struggling with retaining the authenticity of their identity this is a worldwide phenomenon. And, we're back at the seat of it especially with the refugee crisis in the world. What we all ought to do is to really try to help each other understand and connect to the authentic voices in our languages. I thank my ancestors for persisting and this is what we must do—persist and insist on using our mother tongue because together when we affirm our identity, we affirm the identity of others.

## COMING TO AMERICA

*Jesusita Valencia, age 81, Female*
*Birthplace–Cali, Colombia*
*Occupation–Seamstress (Retired)*
*Mother Tongue: Spanish*
*Speaks: American English*

*Margie: Describe your life in Colombia.*
My mother died when I was 8 years old. For the first 2 years I went to live with my father and stepmother. Afterwards I was raised by my grandmother. At 12 years old I met a family of sisters who became my friends for life.

When I got married to my husband he had one more year of college. After he finished, he and his friend started a business in Cali. My husband was a mechanical industrial engineer who made wrought iron fences. He was independent and he wanted his own business so he branched off from his friend and started his own business in my father's garage. He bought some machines and things went well for a while. We were having our children then, four in all so I was at home with them. In the meantime Fanny, one of the sisters from the family of sisters I grew up with was doing contract work in the States where she lived in New York City. It was common for Colombian women to work as maids in the United States under a contract. Once the contract was fulfilled they gained legal status and were allowed to remain in America as residents.

After a while the steel industry went into decline and it became harder to get the materials necessary to make the fences so my husband's business began to suffer. My husband wanted to leave Colombia because of the bad economy but we had not decided where we would go. America became the choice after we visited the consulate and the line for the United States was short. Plus, I did miss my friends dearly and wanted to be near them in New York City. I came to America with my young daughter, Myriam on December 3, 1961 with plans for my husband and other children to follow. My husband found employment quickly when he entered the States and he eventually earned a degree in Mechanical Engineering from Queens College.

*Margie: When you came to America did you live in a Spanish speaking neighborhood?*
Jesusita: No. Jewish and Italian neighborhood.

*Margie: How did you learn English?*
Jesusita: When I started to work at the factory in New York City. My friend told me in America all of the women work. So, back then the tall buildings in New York had factories on every floor so I would wait downstairs until I see a group of women then I asked if they spoke Spanish, when they said yes then I would say, "do you know if anyone has a job?" "Yeah sure, take the elevator to the $8^{th}$ floor." My friend taught me how to say in English, "You have a job for me?" and "I'm looking for work." That's how I started learning English for my job.

But wait. I have a big story for you. When me and my husband went to the consulate we had to show $250 to get the green card, to prove we could take care of ourselves in America. That was a lot of money. [Starts to cry] I was to send the money back to my husband so that he could follow me by doing the same thing. My friend Fanny said, "no, don't send back everything." And she took me shopping to buy a winter coat, boots, sweater, hat and gloves. I dressed very well for winter. [Starts to cry again] then I sent what money was left back to my husband so that he and my other children could join me.

Work was unstable at the factory. The company may have a big order to ship out so they need extra workers but only for four weeks then they let you go and then you have to go find work again. I went to Amirah and she said, "don't worry we'll find you another job." Her Dominican friend took me to her factory and they loved me there because my line is very straight and I can sew fast. I used to take the train with her every day but one day she got sick and I had to go to work alone. Oh, boy! I got lost coming back home. I got off at the wrong stop and there was no one in the station. I was frightened and scared. Then I took out all of my papers, my passport and green card to look for the telephone number. I left my papers at the train station. Then a man came but he didn't speak Spanish but I could tell by his body language that he was telling me to wait because he had called the police. When the police officer came he was Irish, so we still couldn't communicate. Then a Puerto Rican man came along and I told him my story in Spanish. He volunteered to ride the train with me to my stop. When I came out of the train station I started seeing familiar things. The man was kind enough to walk me all the way to my house then he gave me a big hug goodbye. The Puerto Ricans did this a lot for the new people [Hispanic immigrants] moving into the city.

I started working with Italians and Jewish people in the factories because a Puerto Rican woman I know who spoke English too said to me, "if you want to learn English don't work around Spanish speaking people." She said, "try to work with Italians and Jewish people because the Black Americans don't work in the factories. They worked for the government or for the trains." She told me when I'm sewing close my eyes and listen to the conversation that is going on around me in English–when they say something like, "I'm tired" repeat the words to yourself and then when you go home ask someone who knows English what does that mean? I'm tired." My children were beginning to speak English so I could ask them. I didn't allow my daughters to go over to other people's houses but they were welcome to have company. One of their English speaking girlfriends was over and they were in the bedroom talking about a boy. I hollered from my bedroom, I hear what you're saying. They were surprised. They said, "Oh, mommy understands English." So that's how I learned by listening. I look at television too which helps me like now on channel 13. I watch *Kelly and Mike* every morning.

*Margie: Tell me why you and your husband insisted that your children speak Spanish only in the home.*

Jesusita: Because it is the native tongue. At the time we didn't know English. Also, I had some Italian friends who were much older than me influence my decision. They had been in America longer than me and they warned me not to stop the Spanish because they said in three months my children would be speaking English anyway and if I didn't do something they would forget the mother tongue. We didn't want that for our family.

## SALSA IN THE AFTERNOON

*Vilma Valencia, age 57, Female*
*Birthplace–Cali, Colombia*
*Occupation –Medical Esthetician*
*Mother Tongue: Spanish*
*Speaks: American English, Spanish*

My parents brought me to America from Colombia in the early 1960s. My father, a design engineer, had to prove to the United States government that he had enough money and the means to earn more money to take care of his family of five before we were allowed entry. My mother is a seamstress. When I started school in America, it was earth-shattering to be the only Black girl picked out of class daily to go take ESL lessons. Twenty pairs of eyes would fall on me; the weight was too much to bear. I stuck with it until I mastered English. My confidence level rose as I began to learn to speak English and could move between it and Spanish comfortably.

These days I live on both sides of a red velvet curtain. During the day, when the curtain goes up I am fluent in English. I work as a healthcare professional at a doctor's office. This particular scene calls for me to play before strict audiences who demand English only. It's not hard to do and I *break a leg* because my graceful moves are without seams. At times, I receive loud applause and give an encore performance by working late at the office, but as the curtain comes down I am fluent Spanish as it's briskly ushered from the wings. It takes a bold stroll across the stage following me to my dressing room at the precise moment I step foot inside of my home which I share with my elderly parents and where we maintain a strict house rule— NO ENGLISH. Spanish spills from our TVs and radios and is at the center of our family conversations, and when we talk on the telephone.

At work I meet regularly with pharmaceutical sales representatives. There's a woman in particular, a white Anglo-Saxon whom I meet with often. Our interaction is cordial and professional but noticeably distant. She usually comes alone but on one particular visit to the office she brought her manager with her a man, who at first glance I couldn't tell was Hispanic but when she introduced him to me as John Perez I greeted him in Spanish.

"*Como estas soy Colombiana but I was raised in New York City*" (How are you? I'm from Colombia). His shoulders relaxed and he gave me a familiar smile as he spoke back to me in Spanish. With nothing else for the woman to go on but my unruly brush of curly black hair and dark bronze colored skin she looked at me in mild shock and exclaimed, "Valencia, I thought you were Black-American. I didn't know you were Spanish!" The room stopped momentarily to breathe. I've seen this look come across the faces of people in America before. Black, white and others. It somehow says,

"Oh, I thought you were a regular nigger." I simply smiled back at her as we carried on with the business of stocking the reception area.

Out of nowhere John asked me playfully in English, "How well can you salsa?" He put his stack of pamphlets down on the table, smiled at me warmly and extended his hand where I took it in mine. He placed his other hand on the small of my back and we did a simple salsa turn. We laughed together as we stood splitting the sun filtering into the room spinning lightly on the carpet in the middle of the afternoon, as we danced to the rhythm of imaginary salsa beats imprinted on the part of our brain that carries the cultural memory of a people. Since then whenever the woman visits the office she's more at ease with me, our exchange is friendlier, and her guard is down.

I think having the ability to speak more than one language has its advantages in a society where its citizens speak one dominant language because it allows me the freedom to access a variety of cultures and verbal expressions. It seems it gives me a deeper insight into the kaleidoscope of humanity. I have discovered about myself that I have an affinity for learning and speaking other languages. In America, I claim friends who come from all parts of the world. With each encounter, I insist that my friends teach me something about their language and culture and I teach them about mine. Some of my friends are like me, truly bilingual, and there are others who struggle to build a bridge between their first language and English. For us, learning English has been a song where the melody is soft, cautious, and deliberate.

## AMERICA HERE I AM

*Name: Myriam Quinones, Age 62, Female*
*Occupation: Multi-systemic Therapist*
*Mother Tongue: Spanish*
*Speaks: American English*

*Margie: Tell me about your family background.*
Myriam: I was born in Cali, Colombia and came to the U.S. in December of 1961. I have three siblings, George, Harold and Vilma. For the most part mom was a stay at home mom and dad traveled. Mom was the disciplinary. Dad spend quality time when home involved with family activities. We traveled to South America as a family yearly. And dad and mom exposed us to cultural events in New York as well as allowing us to participate in recreational social activities

*Margie: Tell me how you came to be in the United States. Provide as much description as possible.*

Myriam: My parents came for vacation and at the time it was easy to get the status of residence. My Dad went to the United States consulate and inquired about the process. Dad had no clue what residential status meant so he went to my mom's father for advice. My grandfather told my dad, "Son even if you are going to the United States of America you will not be a full citizen if you do not accept residency status." Dad signed up for residency instead as visiting and we all came to the U.S. with residence status. Mom and I came in December and my siblings came in April of 1962. We lived in New York with my parent's childhood friends who convinced dad to stay and he immediately found employment.

*Margie: What are your experiences speaking your mother tongue in a multicultural society?*
Myriam: It was easy at the time as learning a new language came easy to me. I can recall having a Jewish boy assigned to me in class. He would point to things and sound out the words to me. Public schools at that time did not have English as a Second Language instruction.

*Margie: Describe for me the difference between speaking your mother tongue in America and speaking it at home or with family members.*
Myriam: Colombians pattern their tone and expressions after the Spaniards pattern of speaking Spanish. Many believe this is the proper way of speaking Spanish. However, this can be very debatable as there is different dialogue going on about the Spanish language.

*Margie: Describe for me the times you've had to help someone maybe in your community or workplace with language, either mother tongue or another language.*
Myriam: In my work place Spanish is essential because my job requires me to interact with Hispanics from all walks of life.

*Margie: What have you done to become fluent in English or any other language?*
Myriam: I learned English as a child.

*Margie: Why is speaking English important especially if you live and work in America?*
Myriam: It is the mother tongue of this country and speaking English helps in advancing in your profession.

*Margie: Tell me about your experience with learning a new language.*

Myriam: Hard to remember because I was very young; however, the experience was that the people around me were willing to help and were very patient with me

*Margie: Why is speaking your mother tongue is important to you?*
Myriam: It is important to speak my mother tongue because it is part of my culture. With that being said it has made me ensure that my children speak Spanish. Both of my children Tatiana and Don were born in Texas and they speak Spanish fluently. Language is a connection to the culture which is important to me and my family.

*Margie: How does your family feel about your work?*
Myriam: My family members are hard workers and are invested in excelling in their chosen field.

*Margie: What is your attitude towards people who speak English well?*
Myriam: I am impressed and would like to emulate them.

*Margie: What is your attitude towards people who do not speak English well?*
Myriam: I am nonjudgmental.

*Margie: What would cause you to lose your mother tongue?*
Myriam: Nothing. I continue to excel and put into practice my Spanish. My grandchild is one years old and we are teaching her Spanish as the family speaks to her in Spanish as well as her babysitter.

## BLACKS SPEAK SPANISH TOO

*Name: Harold "Paco" Valencia*
*Age: 55, Male*
*Occupation: Organization Development Consultant*
*Birthplace: Cali, Colombia*
*Mother Tongue: Spanish*
*Speaks: American English*

*Margie: Tell be a bit about your family background.*
Harold: I am a Black man born in Cali, Colombia, South America. I came to America in 1962 with my father, brother and sister. My oldest sister and my mother arrived several months earlier. My father told me that the economy in Colombia was bad so he decided to sell his business and find another place to live that would offer his children more opportunities than he had for work and education. He narrowed it down to two countries: Venezuela and

the United States. It seems, at that time, not many people were immigrating to the U.S. because when my father arrived at the consulate's office, there were long lines in the Venezuelan office and the United States' office was empty. He took this as a sign that he should go to America. The greatest motivating factor however, was that he and my mother had close friends who had already moved to America a year prior. Particularly there were five women whom my mother was raised with in Colombia. She missed them dearly and wanted to be near them.

*Margie: What are your experiences speaking your mother tongue in a multicultural society?*
Harold: I was raised in Brooklyn, New York and my community was very diverse with the exception of white people. Additionally, there were very few people like me. I am Black and speak Spanish fluently. The brothers [African Americans] don't embrace me wholeheartedly because I speak Spanish and the Spanish people don't embrace me wholeheartedly because I am Black. Needless to say, whenever I speak Spanish everyone is in shock.

I had one experience where I was talking to my mother on a pay phone back when pay phones existed. A brother walks up to me and asks, "What kind of nigga are you?" I didn't experience him as being malicious; I saw that he was just curious because he had never seen a black man speak Spanish so fluently. While out in public, I'll speak to a Spanish person in Spanish and they look at me in amazement and always ask me where did I learn to speak Spanish? Ninety-five percent of the time they tell me that I'm lying. Some ask which of my parents are black and I proudly tell them both of them are black and they both speak Spanish.

White people, in-turn, are pleasantly surprised that I speak Spanish and they treat me like they would any other black person. I get discriminated in the same way as any other black man in the United States. I feel and have experienced the prejudicial and discriminatory difference between being a white Hispanic and a black Hispanic in the U.S. While serving in the United States Navy, people who did not speak Spanish did not want me to speak Spanish in their presence. Many felt that I was talking about them to my Spanish brothers and sisters. Actually, sometimes I was talking about them. Speaking a different language has its advantages.

*Margie: Describe for me the times you've had to help someone maybe in your community or workplace with language, either mother tongue or another language.*
Harold: I was in the grocery store and over the loudspeaker the store manager asked if someone could speak Spanish and interpret at the pharmacy counter. When I walked up and introduced myself, one of the black employees did not believe that I could speak Spanish. She turned and asked my wife,

who has a light complexion, did she teach me how to speak Spanish. I took the opportunity to educate the woman and let her know that there are black people all over the world and that slavery did not only take place in America! While in the military, the commanding officer utilized my talents and had me serve as an interpreter when we would visit Spanish speaking countries. On a side note, my boot camp company commander would make me count off my push-ups in Spanish. I felt proud because this was a way to let the others know that I was a Spanish Black Man.

*Margie: What have you done to become fluent in English or any other language?*
Harold: I came here at two years old and learned English in school. I started school at the age of 5 years old and I remember that although I had been in America for three years. I didn't know how to speak English when it was time to start school. Everyone in my family spoke Spanish so I didn't learn English prior to starting school. There weren't English as a second language classes so I was placed in the class with the retarded children. I quickly learned English and was removed from that classroom and was ultimately placed in the classes for students with the highest GPA's at the school.

*Margie: Why is speaking English important especially if you live and work in America?*
You should learn English out of respect for the country. People need to try their best to learn the language of the country they live in.

*Margie: Tell me about your experience with learning a new language.*
Harold: I was too young and don't quite remember how it felt to learn English. I do remember friends laughing at me when I pronounced words with a Spanish accent. I can't say that I intentionally lost my accent but I think I lost my accent somewhere along the way. I speak English with a Brooklyn New York accent. In-fact, some would say that I speak English with a Brooklyn street accent. Which by the way, I am very proud of.

*Margie: Why is speaking your mother tongue is important to you?*
Harold: It's a big part of who I am.

*Margie: How does your family feel about your work?*
My family is very proud of my 25 years of military service and they are equally as proud of my post military career.

*Margie: What is your attitude towards people who speak English well?*

Harold: Effective communication is instrumental in everything we do. The command of the English language opens doors that otherwise will never open.

*Margie: What is your attitude towards people who do not speak English well?*

Live and let live! On the other hand, if you work in this country then you should try your best to continuously improve your ability to speak English. In terms of progress, if you are trying to climb the ladder of success in this country, you had better learn the language.

*Margie: What would cause you to lose your mother tongue?*
Harold: Death.

*Margie: If you have children (or when you have children) will you teach them your mother tongue? Why or Why not?*

I served for 25 years in the U.S. Navy and I was married to a woman who did not speak Spanish. It was easier for me to speak English with my wife and children than to speak one language to the kids and a different language to my wife. Hence the children did not learn Spanish. As they grew older and were exposed to my side of the family, they expressed some interest. My youngest daughter, Taylor, took it upon herself to learn and now speaks English and Spanish fluently and most recently added Thai to her repertoire. My oldest, Brandi, understands quite a bit of Spanish and puts a few phrases together from time to time. I'm very pleased to say that both of my daughters and my wife love Spanish music.

*Margie: This is the end of the interview. Is there anything else you would like to share on topic or off topic?*

Harold: Nobody wants to be Black. As a child, I felt torn between Black people and white Spanish people. Again, the Blacks did not accept me 100% because I spoke Spanish and the Spanish did not accept me 100% because I was Black. As I grew older, I felt more accepted by the Blacks and felt more comfortable around people who looked like me. While growing up and becoming a young man, the only people around me that looked like me and experienced discrimination and prejudice the way I did were Black Americans. Once I became a man, I noticed that more and more people of color who come from other countries want to make it clear that they are not Black. It's almost as if no one wants to be black (Black-American), not realizing that if it was not for the African-American, the privileges people of color experience in the United States would not exist today, which rides on the backs of thousands of slaves and their descendants!

## BEATING THE ODDS

*George Valencia, Age 59, Male*
*Occupation: NYPD (ret.), US Coast Guard (ret.)*
*Birthplace: Cali, Colombia*
*Mother Tongue: Spanish*
*Speaks: American English*

My father brought us to the United States in 1963, where we were raised in Brooklyn. I started public school and I didn't speak any English. I was very scared because it was a culture shock to me at four years old. I learned the English language very fast. My school-teacher was so impressed that she actually had my mother come to the school to acknowledge my accomplishment. As time progressed, I became accustomed to the United States but being bilingual we were not allowed to speak English at home. So when we came home from school we had to speak Spanish in the house and at home it was strictly Spanish and in the streets with my friends it was English so I was raised extremely bilingual.

The culture of being dark skinned Black Hispanic made my identity process weird because people at that time didn't understand how someone of color could speak Spanish. So, we would have to explain to them that in South America there are people of color who speak Spanish. They just didn't know. People would be amazed, "Oh, you speak Spanish?" So, I grew up with that in New York. I grew accustomed to it.

In high school I played sports and I was also a musician. I played Latin jazz. Growing up in New York I played with bands since I was fourteen years old. My mother brought me a guitar and I learned to play it. I used to play in soul bands like the James Brown music, the Stylistics and the Delphonics. I was always the isolated child because I was in to music. Of course my siblings got into other things. As I grew older I started playing more instruments. I found a piano and an organ in the street and I started practicing every day on them at home in the basement for about a year. My neighbor heard me playing and asked my mother who was that playing that beautiful piano? My mom told her it was her son tinkering. The neighbor said, "no he plays good. I know a salsa band that's looking for a piano player." I said, "no, no. I'm not ready to play with a big band." The next thing you know I went and bought an electric piano and I did go play with that big salsa band in Brooklyn and Red Hook. We travelled and toured the country for three years.

I got married to my high school sweetheart five years after we got out of high school and I was still with the band and working menial jobs. We got married at the age of 24 and life was pleasant. My band played at my wedding but then my wife started giving me a hard time so I didn't play as much.

I decided to stick with the marriage. My wife started working at Pfizer Pharmaceutical and then she got me a job there too. We just grew together. We decided to go back to school for ultra sound. Then I applied to the police department. It was a hard process to get in being a minority it's hard to get in. I applied in 1981 and it took me five years to get in. I was so ecstatic it was a good job, it was a good paying job. The force was predominantly Irish and Italian. Blacks are a minority and here I was a Black Hispanic. They started giving me a hard time being from Colombia and I had to become a citizen. I got on the job and I beat the odds again. So, I had two professions at the time. I was doing ultra sound on the side and working at the police department full-time. My wife and I did very well. We lived in the nice part of Brooklyn and after being on the force for three years we beat the odds again and bought a house on Long Island in the suburbs. A more upper class neighborhood. And we were 31, young with our own beautiful home.

My kids were little, they were one and three. My wife was working for the police department too. She was a 911 operator but once we moved to Long Island my wife had to quit the police department because of a residency requirement. She left and went to work as a bookkeeper at Sieman's Funiture. She went back to school and got her associate's degree. Then she got her BS from Malloy College; it's a small woman's college. Then I joined the United States Coast Guard in 1990. Again I beat the odds because they told me I wasn't going to make it because it was a completely white organization. I went to the academy and graduated from my class as a third class. I never in my wildest dreams thought I would be a chief in the Coast Guard because I was Black! I did both careers together and I excelled in both.

I retired from the NYPD in 2004. I got hurt because I'm a 9/11 survivor. I was in the south tower when the towers came down. I'll save that story for another time. I have spoken about my experiences at many engagements. My wife and I decided to relocate to Houston from New York. My wife left first. I was very sick after 9/11 so I got out of the military for a year. I got myself back on track with medications for PTSD. My wife then decided to go back to school to get her Master's in business. Guess who paid for that education? The United States Coast Guard so it worked out just fine. As time went on my kids were becoming older (inaudible) one day my son told me he wanted to follow in my foot steps and become a police officer. Bilingual mind you. He is third generation who still speaks Spanish in our family. They listened to the salsa and Latin music like you hear now. At home I only spoke Spanish to my children.

Mind you my son worked as a security guard for a private security firm at Verizon and then one day Verizon asked him to quit that security job and come to work for them because they would ask him to translate for the Mexicans who would come in...(trails off) they always called on him to translate. He got a raise in the new position. My daughter graduated from

Texas A&M with a degree in criminal psychology and she decided to be a school teacher. She is also bilingual, we kept it third generation my daughter has decided to bring what she learned from her degree and she wants to be a lawyer. She also wants to follow in my footsteps and her brother's so she applied for the Houston Police Department. They did give her a hard time because she's a woman and Black. She tried three times and didn't make it but I encouraged her by telling her that in life you don't give up until you fall and you can't get back up. I told her if you can't get back up than the only one who can get you up is God. If you fall and can't get back up than it's because you didn't want to get back up. She listened to me and she tried again and passed with flying colors so now she begins the academy February 14, 2016.

My wife got her Master's degree and decided to open up a business. She learned from a mentor who she paid to help get her started; a Jewish woman who had her own business worked with my wife for a whole year. My wife being Hispanic she was very scared because the business is predominantly white. But, my wife beat the odds again and opened up her own business and it exploded and now her patients are doctors and lawyers and people from all different races who come to her and she can speak perfect Spanish to the Hispanic patients who need ultra sound so her business is prospering.

I retired from the police department and I continued on with the Coast Guard. While living in Houston I became chief in 2009 I was assigned Prevention Chief in the Port of Houston. I was sent to school for training and I was given 15 people in my unit under my command which did facility inspection for the Coast Guard.

*Margie: Why is speaking your mother tongue important to you?*

George: I'm going to make you laugh but speaking my mother tongue was very important to me because my mother wouldn't respond in any other language. [Laughter] It was mandatory for me to learn it. If you wanted to ask for --back then it was a dime or a quarter for candy-- or if I wanted to say, "Mommy my tummy hurts," I had better say it in Spanish [Laughter]. She wouldn't even look at you if it was in English. We had to learn the rough, tough hard way. Now when my friends came over and rang the bell it was in English but when you opened my door to my house it was going into another culture. We lived extremely bilingual and then my mother taught us how to read and write it [Spanish] on the weekends. She gave us classes. Then also I married a Hispanic woman, my wife is from Puerto Rico. Being bilingual has helped me survive the melting pot because we had to learn English but the Spanish helped us get on both sides of the road. Whenever one of us got a job it's like, "oh you speak Spanish? Then we need you over here." Even in the police department I was used constantly to translate for prisoners arrested who didn't speak English

*Margie: Ok. This ends the interview. Before I turn the tape off is there anything else you would like to share on topic or off topic?*

George: On topic I didn't know what my advancement in the Coast Guard meant until I was called for that big oil spill in the Gulf of Mexico. I was called for that oil spill. That made me see life at its best. I went to Louisiana where I was activated with the military I went there as a chief and when I get there I'm the only Black Hispanic chief there everybody else there was white and so it put me in a culture shock again because I was in the Coast Guard for 25 years and (inaudible) I was well respected and treated as royalty. I couldn't believe I had reached this epitome in my life. I felt special [he extends his arms like a bird in flight and gives a great big smile] because I was a chief I had a separate hotel room and my own driver. I was there for two months and I met people from all over the world and I made beautiful friends for life. This experience showed me the reward of what it's like going through the ranks and achieving success. I saw the respect that was given me and I thought about my father bringing us here in 1963 holding our little hands and going to a country where we didn't know what to expect and here we are. We completely took advantage of the system.

Jorge Valencia's passport.

Jorge and Jesusita Valencia at a friend's party circa, 2000.

Four generations of Valencia women taken in Houston, TX, in 2015.

Harold Valencia United States Navy Photo taken in 1999.

Margie and George Valencia taken in Houston, TX, in 2015.

Yonas A., born in Addis Ababa, Ethiopia.

Tu Anh P. with children in his home village Dong Thap Province.

# Section 2
# Mother Tongue American Style

". . . my first language was Hawaii Creole, a language that was created by the children of plantation workers and used by later generations as an everyday common language. Although I could write in Standard English, I had difficulty speaking it spontaneously. Before expressing my thoughts, I had to translate them from Hawaii Creole to Standard English. Often, by the time I was ready to speak, someone else had said what I had intended to say . . ."—Eileen H. Tamura

### THE CULTURE BEARER

*Tu Anh P., age 24, Male*
*Birthplace – Dorchester, MA*
*Occupation – Community Organizer*
*Mother Tongue: Vietnamese*
*Speaks: American English, Vietnamese*

*Author's Note: I met Tu at a poetry reading in Roxbury, MA. After he read his poem, "Chakras of Refugee Embodiment or 7 Ways to Love Your Asian Body" I asked him for an interview. Tu's poem is included in Appendix A.*

Let's begin with my family. I'm the youngest of six siblings. My family immigrated to Boston in 1989 right before I was born. Before then we lived in southern Viet Nam and for six months we stayed at a refugee camp in the Philippines before coming to America. The refugee camp is for people who have to leave their countries for different reasons. It's like a culture camp where they teach English and different ways of being American. This is where I was conceived. When my mom boarded the plane for America she was already pregnant with me. Since we are an immigrant family we are very close knit. We grew up speaking Vietnamese in our house all of the time. My closest sibling is seven years older than me. I grew up with two brothers who were my best friends.

Our first house was at Field's Corner which is a neighborhood of Dorchester where there's a huge Vietnamese population. It's where most of the Vietnamese immigrants reside when they come to Boston. Since it was a thriving community with supermarkets, restaurants and everything else you needed my parents didn't feel the need to learn English in order to advance. Growing up I was grounded in Vietnamese culture. As I got older my siblings got married and moved out because there was no space. At one point we had ten people living in our apartment. My siblings weren't necessarily educated--none of them went to college. They worked menial jobs and moved out of the city because it was more affordable. Suddenly, my house became just my parents and me. I remember not being able to communicate with them mostly because I wasn't home as much. No one was home.

I started learning English when I was in kindergarten. I was put in a Catholic school in Field's Corner and my family is Buddhist [Laughter]. My parents had heard in the community that public schools were really bad so they spent money so that I could go to Catholic school. I attended with my two nephews who are close to my age. We treat each other as if we're cousins. I remember being so lost at school because I didn't know English at that point. In the church we had Mass and it was a really weird experience too. I remember struggling and I remember being quiet all of the time because I really didn't know what was going on and it was my first experience with school and being away from home. Also, I had been given an American name, which I was not used to hearing, which was Tony. I never chose it. My mom chose it for me. So, growing up I had the name 'Tony'. There're people from my street where I grew up who still call me Tony. But, as I got older around the time of middle school I rejected my American name.

"This is not my name. At home my name is Tu [pronounced Too]", I would say to others. My older brothers chose their names. Their official government names are Tommy and Tyson, which they had to go through a legal process for this name change. I think their experience was: How do I become more Americanized? For me it was and is the opposite effect. I wanted to embrace my Vietnamese culture because I felt like that was my connection to home.

As I got older I was really into hip-hop and I began losing my Vietnamese. I wasn't speaking it at home because all of my siblings had moved out and now I was speaking English to my parents. Even when my siblings did come around we would practice English by speaking it more to each other because it's very useful. Sometimes we talk between both languages depending on the situation. If we are at family gatherings it will be mostly Vietnamese. If the interaction is more interpersonal, just day-to-day, it's a push and pull between English and Vietnamese.

In the last year, I've become more aware of my identity as a Vietnamese-American and I feel very comfortable with the fact that I'm able to represent my Vietnamese heritage. My job is really rewarding because I get to talk to Vietnamese elders and train other young people on how to talk to the elders so that we can we can organize them around issues important to the community. I never had Vietnamese friends growing up and I find that the Vietnamese-Americans I work with who are my own age also struggle with their language. Out of the group I'm one of the more proficient Vietnamese speakers. It has been a bit of a challenge engaging the young people into talking to the elders, most of whom don't speak English, in Vietnamese. The struggle of my peers is apparent as they search for a voice they've lost in their American homes. You can gauge their body language. There's such a need to speak the language that they're finding different ways to reacquire it and use it more often.

My hugest influence for keeping my language happened when I was 15 years old. It was on my fourth trip back to Viet Nam where we have lots of family. I had this experience there where all my neighbors were making fun of me because of the way I spoke Vietnamese. They said, "you can't speak Vietnamese" and "it's really bad." At the time I was used to speaking Vietnamese only to my family in America so I never had much practice. My Vietnamese was kind of broken but I was trying to fit in. It was really embarrassing and I felt ashamed of myself. When I returned to America I said to myself, "I need to stay Vietnamese and keep my language." Our family goes back to Viet Nam regularly and it is important to me that I'm able to speak the language. I held on to Vietnamese because there are just some things which can't be translated in English that I want to express. I think my whole life has been me trying to find a voice and trying to find a way to articulate those feelings. Sometimes I think of things in Vietnamese words but I don't have the necessary language to really say it in English so constantly I struggle with just being able to talk to people.

I want to tell you what I'm going through right now where language is concerned. Now that I'm older my family has grown to where I have a total of fifteen nieces and nephews who were born and raised in America. These younger members of my family are at varying stages with the language—some of them speak Vietnamese really well because they have been trained by their parents to; there are others who never learned to speak Vietnamese especially if their parents only speak English to them at home; some speak very little Vietnamese, while the rest understand it a little bit. This causes great confusion for children especially when they're trying to gauge how much Vietnamese they need to know so that they can understand what a family member is saying at a gathering versus how much English they need to know in order to be a successful citizen.

I call myself the 1.5 generation, because even though I grew up in America, my family is so Vietnamese, making that a great part of my identity too. These unique experiences together allow me to relate more deeply to my nieces and nephews than can older members of my family. I see my role with them as the culture bearer. Language is really important. I have this fear that if we lose Vietnamese we will lose our culture. I don't want this to happen. I'm always quick to talk to my nieces and nephews about my position on this subject. And, when I do talk to them I speak in Vietnamese and in English. I think if I were to have children of my own one day they would learn English naturally. Teaching them Vietnamese would be a challenge but I feel it would be important to let them know that there are other ways in which to express yourself. I would keep them mindful of where we come from and teach them about our ancestors and our language.

I've been writing poetry for about eight years. I'm still struggling to learn how to write Vietnamese. The longest thing I've ever written in Vietnamese was a letter to a friend in Viet Nam. It took a long time for me to write trying to get the accent marks right. [Laughter] But, I do occasionally use Vietnamese phrases in my work. I have this one poem I wrote while travelling throughout Southeast Asia. When people greet each other there they don't say, 'how are you?' There's no phrase for that. Instead we greet each other by saying, *"An com trua?"* which means "have you eaten rice yet?" This lets me know right away that my culture is connected to food and is concerned with the well-being of family, friends and neighbors.

## SPANISH AMERICAN STYLE

*Alice E., age 57, Female*
*Birthplace –Los Angeles, CA*
*Occupation –Dental Assistant (Retired)*
*Mother Tongue: American English*
*Speaks: Spanish*

*Anthony E., age 63, Male*
*Birthplace- Los Angeles, CA*
*Occupation – Auto Maker*
*Mother Tongue: American English*
*Speaks: Broken Spanish*

*Author's Note: I met Alice and Anthony while they were vacationing at Graceland. They were taking a break from the tour to have ice-cream and agreed to be interviewed.*

*Margie: What is your experience speaking Spanish in a multicultural society?*

Alice: Sometimes people are very skeptical because they don't understand what we're saying which is why a lot of times I won't speak Spanish unless I'm speaking to someone who can understand what I'm saying. I know when I go places and if people are speaking a language I don't understand it makes me feel uncomfortable. I try not to do that--to make people feel uncomfortable.

*Margie: Can you tell me your story?*

Alice: My husband and I got married on June 24, 1978 and we both came from Los Angeles..[Pauses]

Anthony: Let me tell you what the story is. I was raised by my mother who was an orphan in Arizona. My father was born in Santa Monica and although both came from Hispanic backgrounds my parents didn't raise us to speak Spanish. We were raised to speak English. My father told me that we were raised to speak English so that we could compete against the white person and the way to do that was to get educated so that we could compete in a white world. Being brown and Hispanic we looked different, we spoke different, we had a different culture, we ate different foods and they didn't believe we would have the same opportunities as whites if we were uneducated. We learned to read it, write it, and we learned to compete. My brother and sister and even I became very successful because we were raised this way. My brother is a school teacher, raised to be a Catholic priest. My sister is a nurse. I was a mortician. Also, I went to school 3 years pre-med in nursing college, which I got out of because I didn't want to do it anymore. I eventually got into the auto industry after earning a four year engineering degree. The whole key is education. And that's the same thing I stress to my daughters and to my grandkids is education. If you're going to get ahead in the world you have to have an education.

*Margie: Do you have a similar story, Alice?*

Alice: The way we got our Hispanic background is that my grandparents were from Mexico. My mom's parents were from Mexico but my dad's parents were from Texas. So, from my understanding my grandfather on my mom's side brought them to America to seek better opportunities for work. I learned the Spanish from my aunts. When they would all get together they would speak English and as soon as they started speaking Spanish we all knew the story had to be a juicy one. My grandmother died when I was really young but my grandfather spoke only Spanish and broken English. It was my uncle who would push us to speak the language of the Mexicans and that we needed to know a different language [other than English] and that as we grew up if would be beneficial. Our family believed different than what my husband's family believed, especially if you were a woman, my father just didn't want to spend any money on us going to college. So, if you wanted to go to school you went to learn a trade.

Margie: *When do you have opportunities to speak Spanish in our multicultural society?*
Anthony: I think it was a great injustice for my parents not to speak Spanish to us at home because it's always better to know two languages. You know, when I worked at GM, I worked around a lot of Mexican people. One guy told me this story about two mice who were trapped by a cat in the corner. They looked at each other and said, "What are we going to do?" The one mouse say to the other, "I'll tell you what I'm going to do." He looked straight at the cat and in his loudest voice he said, "Woof!, Woof!" The cat turned around and ran away. The other mouse was impressed and said, "Where did you learn to do that? The mouse said, "it's always nice to know two languages!" I never forgot that joke and I thought that was a good idea so when we got married I have had my wife to teach me Spanish throughout the years.

Alice: All of that [Spanish] on my side pretty much died out when my grandparents passed away.

## A WORK IN PROGRESS

*Israel P., Age 26, Male*
*Occupation: Receptionist/Student*
*Birthplace: Los Angeles, CA*
*Mother Tongue: Spanish*
*Speaks: American English, French, Mandarin*

My mother was born in a country called El Salvador in Central America and she immigrated here in 1986, the year the Challenger exploded. My father was born in Bolivia in South America. He and my mother met in America and had me. He later went back to his home country and I stayed here with my mother. I'm an only child. Growing up the primary language and the only source of communication between my mother and me was Spanish. I learned English later at school.

With all of my friends we speak English to each other, even my friends whose parents speak Spanish. They too will speak only Spanish to their parents but when it comes to us talking to each other we speak English.

When it comes to occupation it's always been English although I acquired a job in Memphis that allows me to speak some Spanish because the owners and the managers are Spanish and most of the employees are too.

I help my mother all of the time, when she's confused or shy about speaking to somebody in English I step in. When it comes to Spanish maybe a couple is in a restaurant or grocery store and somebody's speaking English to them and they don't know what's going on so again I step in and say something. It feels good whenever I help someone. I think I do it because I understand how it is going somewhere and not having a clue as to what's going on with the language. It can be difficult. I've seen my mother go through it and I feel if I'm in a position to help so, why not?

Speaking my mother tongue is important to me because I hear people in college say that speaking another language utilizes your brain in a different way. Another thing is I feel like it's a gift that has been given to me and I should learn to cultivate this free gift. Many people are born with different gifts and if you have one you must cultivate it.

I moved out of the house at 18 and living on my own I noticed that my Spanish wasn't that good. I had issues with the reading and writing so I've been working on that little by little. Of course living in America you only speak English. I was never really integrated into a Spanish community or the places I chose to live were not really Spanish speaking communities so there was no utilization of Spanish although I saw Spanish as a tool at my disposal. I needed to keep up with so I kept up with it by reading and listening to movies and music just to keep my brain refreshed.

Among my colleagues and Latino friends we speak a code that uses Spanish words in a conversation of English to get our point across. I have read several articles about this type of conversation among Latino Americans and have come to the conclusion that we do this because there are meanings and emotions we would like to communicate that do not quite have an equivalent in English. I think we use these several words in conversation with another who does understand Spanish and the feelings and thoughts a Spanish word would connote when trying to explain oneself.

If I have children in the future I will have them formally educated in Spanish. I've heard that there are some other cultures like Greeks and Italians who will put their children through grammar school to learn that language. I think this is a curious idea because the way I learned Spanish was strictly in the home listening to tones and how it was spoken.

I have applied to a graduate program in Shanghai to study Chinese philosophy. I chose to apply for this program to continue my education in another country both to travel and to study. During undergrad, I studied Chinese to expand my knowledge of languages in order to achieve an understanding of languages and how they work in our communications in daily life. I seek to use this skill to attain a career which will require extensive communication skills in a job such as interpreter or translator of philosophical articles in Chinese. I'm a work-in-progress.

## A HONDURAN BRONX TALE

*Name: Mercy T., Age: 40, Female*
*Occupation: Writer/ Professor / High School English Teacher / Mom*
*Birthplace: New York, NY*
*Mother Tongue: English/Spanish*
*Speaks: American English, Spanish*

I hail from the Bronx, New York City. My parents are from Honduras, Central America. We are Afro-Latinos. My father's folks are from Westmoreland, Jamaica, but moved to Puerto Cortés, Honduras, because of the United Fruit Company (present-day, Chiquita Brands International). As the company was expanding in the early 20th century, workers from the Caribbean were sent to Honduras, Guatemala, and Costa Rica. My paternal grandparents were sent to Honduras during that time. Soon after, my father was born. He has a Honduran birth certificate, but because of his Jamaican parentage, English was his first language.

My mother was derogatorily titled "mulatta," because she was Garifuna (Black) and her father was "Indio," or Native American. Both of my mother's parents were from Belize (British Honduras), but eventually moved to Tela, Honduras, where my mother was born. My father is a Black man, while my mother, being mixed with hair texture that showed the influence of her father, was fully aware of the societal treatments of the people of her appearance, and many times, used that appearance to her advantage.

My mother already had history in the United States because of her first marriage. She had lived in California for some time, then moved back to Honduras when her marriage dissolved. A few years after she met my father and married him, she moved to the Bronx, New York. My father soon followed. He arrived to New York as a first-time tourist with a return ticket, under the expectation of just visiting my mother and hopefully convincing her to come back to Honduras. That return ticket was never used; two weeks into his visit here, he was looking for a job.

When I was young my parents always spoke to me in English. I was born during a time when speaking a language other than English was not acceptable by the overall American culture, so, in my formative years prior to my siblings coming to live with us, my parents and oldest sister made sure I only spoke English. I learned Spanish having to communicate with my siblings. For some time, they did not speak English when they first moved to New York City from Honduras, and just being around them gave me the beginning stages of knowing Spanish. During this time my mother began speaking Spanish to me at home more often.

I think my brain was trying to figure out what was going on. Both languages would come out while I was in school, without my even trying to speak Spanglish. My teachers immediately thought I had a learning disability, and they wanted to put me in special education program. My mother did not sign any papers to allow that to happen, and threatened the school if they put me in special education. She told them that I was acquiring another language at home, and promised them that I would very quickly figure out the language distinction. She was right.

Starting my high school years was when I began to notice I was different from most of the people in my circle. I grew up in a close-knit neighborhood in the Bronx (which, I refer to as "the block"), so we were all seen as individuals with our own histories. I do not recall any experiences of being questioned because we were a Black family who spoke Spanish. I also attended a very small Catholic school on University Avenue in the Bronx, called Holy Spirit School. The graduating 8$^{th}$ grade class was twenty-four students. We all, essentially, grew up together, so my background as an Afro-Latina was never questioned or dismissed.

Outside of my close-knit block and my school, I did definitely experience prejudices. One time, a hairdresser told my mother that he could not work on my hair. Another time, my mother scolded some girls who did not want to let another Black girl play double-dutch, but, because I spoke Spanish, they reluctantly allowed me to play with them. (Of course, my mother did not let me.) But, in my childhood, I never experienced anything that made me question being Black *and* Latina. I grew up eating tortillas, and traditional Honduran/Garifuna dishes. My mother spoke to me more in Spanish. My mother had my hair straightened as soon as I turned 9 years old. My household could not have been any less Latino, and I could not have been any less Black.

When I entered high school, though, my perspective of myself completely changed. I began to question my existence because what I always believed was the truth about me was, for the first time, being challenged. Latino kids did not believe I spoke Spanish. I was like a freak of nature, being put on display. Latinos would gather around me, ask me to say certain words, ask me questions, and they would still not believe that I spoke Spanish. They would tell me that I must have grown-up around a lot of Puerto Ricans, and somehow, managed to get a few words in my vocabulary. Other Black kids would tell me that I was not Black enough. When I tried to be a member of the African American club, I was discouraged because I was told that I was not really Black. Imagine the trying time for me during those high school years. All of my life up until that point, I was able to fit in all of the communities I was a part of. All of a sudden, I was denied acceptance by the same groups I had always identified myself with.

My oldest sister has a memorable story of being in a class soon after she had immigrated from Honduras, and attempted to answer a question that her teacher asked. Because of her accent, the other students laughed at her. The teacher did not stop the other students from laughing; she actually joined them in laughing at her. For my siblings, to be fluent in English was a case of survival. It also meant that knowing the language well did not put them in situations where they would be discriminated against or ridiculed. I cannot recall the length or the efforts involved in my siblings learning Spanish. I do recall not having much of an opportunity to practice my Spanish with them after several months of them moving to New York City.

For my family members, knowing English was what made assimilation possible. They knew America was their new home, so they had to learn the language, and learn it fast. Nowadays, one can go to certain American neighborhoods in big cities with their mother tongue (8th Street in Miami; Washington Heights in New York). When my siblings were growing up as adolescents, they did not have the luxury of going to certain neighborhoods to get items from their home and speak their mother tongue. Learning English was a no-brainer for them.

My mother loved the English language. She was always in a class, wanting to improve her English and wanting to soften her accent to the point of making it disappear. She always had the accent, though, but was able to read English very well and was always able to talk the language understandably well. However, she never really had confidence in her knowledge of English, which is why she was probably always in an English class. Once, she asked me to write an essay for her. I told her I was not going to write the essay, that she needed to write it herself and I would help with editing. She was very upset by my not choosing to write it. She felt it was a personal attack on her, and unwillingness from me to help her. On the contrary; I trusted her ability to write an essay, and I wanted her to see what she was capable of doing.

As for my siblings, they learned English because they had to learn it. I know, at some point, two of my brothers did not feel connected here because they were not learning English well enough and quickly enough. They used to talk about moving back to Honduras. What helped them, I think, is being around other Latinos who were also pulled out of their homes as children and placed in America, under the premise that they needed to sink or swim, and that they should all be grateful they were attending a school in America.

Listening to English language music played a dominant role in helping all of my siblings. I remember listening to Bob Marley, Marvin Gaye, Slick Rick, Run DMC, and Strafe. I also recall listening to Guns N' Roses, Bon Jovi, Pink Floyd, U2 and Hall and Oates. Music was an important part of my upbringing; for my siblings, the music was what helped them improve their English and assimilate American culture.

I worked for the New York City Department of Education for twelve years. I taught English Language Arts to high school students. Some of the parents of my students did not know English; many instances came up with my having to speak in Spanish just to communicate to the parent. What I appreciated about the parents is that they were never surprised that I knew Spanish. I think they were just grateful and happy that someone was able to speak about their child honestly, in their language. I suspect they felt relieved to be able to talk to the teacher of their children one-to-one, adult-to-adult, without the assistance of the child.

Language represents who were are as individuals. I am an adjunct professor of American Literature at the College of New Rochelle; you will find me using double negatives; including curses in my language; throwing some Spanish words in my English sentences, and expecting everyone to understand; and not conjugating my verbs. In other words, I am guilty of code switching. Ideally, we should see the English language as beyond the literal: as long as we are able to understand each other, the grammatical rules should be inconsequential when communicating.

Speaking my mother tongue connects me to my Honduran roots. My mother passed away in 1996; she was the only one who ultimately spoke to me in Spanish more than anyone else. I would, of course, always respond in English. So now, when I talk in Spanish, I am reminded of my mother, Honduras, and being Garifuna. I am reminded of my connection to others who speak Spanish. Although Spanish has just recently been accepted as a legitimate second language to learn, our country always had a necessity to have bilingual workers. My siblings were able to advance in their fields because they knew both Spanish and English equally well. For them, knowing Spanish went from a deterrent to a benefit for employment acquirement and career advancement.

I struggle with keeping my Spanish. I do not really practice it as much as I would like. I do know it is important to me, so I make an effort to keep it fresh in my mind. Also, I definitely want my children to be fluent in Spanish. Now, my son who is in 1st grade at his local public school, takes Spanish classes twice a week! Losing my Spanish is really from not having the language around me much. Whenever I feel disconnected from my family's language, I try to watch a Spanish-language novella. My siblings won't lose their mother tongue because they use it on a regular basis and it helps them financially.

I am 40 years old, and I am now taking my writing seriously. My family members are immigrants, so for them, doing anything artistic was a waste of time and would keep me from earning enough money to support myself. Their focus has always been to get an education, get a 9-5 with benefits, and save money from every check. Because my family struggled financially and socially, doing anything outside of the immigrant prescription of the American Dream would be unacceptable. When any of us came forward, wanting to do something that required uniqueness and artistry, we were laughed at and immediately discouraged. We were taught that we did not have the freedoms that Americans (white people) had, therefore, we could not take certain chances with our lives, the way others so freely did. My father is supportive now; although I wrote stories and poems for as long as I can remember, he is surprised by my talent.

I have absolutely no problem with people speaking with accents, struggling with English. I have a problem with people telling me that my Spanglish is not good enough. I do have a problem with people not choosing to learn English, and still expecting opportunities to be available to them. I have seen my family struggle with learning English, so I feel that while we celebrate the cultures and languages that make our country and culture so beautiful and unique, we must also understand that we must have a common language. The language is a part of our American identity, and we must embrace that in order to be successful as individuals settling in a new land, as a nation and as a whole.

## BLACXICANA

*Nina L., Age 50, Female*
*Occupation: Radio Talk Show Host, Performer and Chef*
*Birthplace: Philadelphia, PA*
*Mother Tongue: English*
*Speaks: American English, Spanish*

I was born in Philadelphia and for the first nine years of my life we spoke English. My father's mother is Mexican. After my grandmother died my father wanted to be closer to his Spanish roots. He tried to convince my mother, his wife with whom he had five children, to move to Mexico, but she was unwilling to leave the country. The compromise was to move to Puerto Rico because it was still a part of the United States and it had a Spanish culture. We moved from Philadelphia in the winter to the tropical blast furnace heat of Puerto Rico. Initially it was very difficult for me because I only spoke two words of Spanish—San Juan—[Laughter]. We started at public school and everything was in Spanish. Eventually we were in bilingual environments for education, but by then I read, wrote and spoke Spanish.

I was considered an outsider when I didn't speak Spanish. I had to learn it quickly. What helped me the most to learn rapidly was watching television where everything was in Spanish. My favorite character was a Mexican actor named Catínflas. I understood visually what was happening, but in order to understand for real, I had to learn the language. I was motivated. After living in Puerto Rico for five years I began to speak and think in Spanish. When I was 14 years old, we moved back to the States and of course I knew English, but I was thinking in Spanish or "Spanglish." It was an initial shock to my system and difficult to go back to speaking English only. It took me about a year or two to adjust.

Speaking Spanish is important to me because it's a good reminder of the cultures and ethnicities that make up my family. Being Black is not monolithic. I call myself Black, but if pushed I say that I am Blacxicana or a Black Mexican. On my mother's side my grandfather was Native American and my grandmother was Gullah/Geechie and on my father's side my grandmother was Mexican and my grandfather was African American. So when I embrace all of my roots I call myself a Blacxicana with indigenous roots.

In the last 15 years, I thought that I had lost my Spanish since I really don't use it as much. But then I took a great journey to Cuba and it all came back to me, instantly. I became the United Nations for my traveling partners, translating on our trip because none of them spoke Spanish. That was exhausting, but I learned, it never goes away. I thought I had lost it because I don't practice daily, but it came right back when I was back in a Spanish speaking country.

My oldest daughter speaks Spanish and my youngest daughter understands it. I think it's really important for children to be multilingual. I think the more languages you speak the better educated you are about the world we live in. I think the more aware you are of your environment the more you can connect to other people. So I make it a point to learn a few words from different languages, so that even if I don't speak it, I can at least greet people or say thank you or have a nice day. I think part of civilization is to be able to communicate with others in their language. It breaks the ice. Language is the key to communicating. I don't necessarily think everyone must speak English, but at the same time I think everyone should be able to communicate in whatever that language is, or the lingua franca is, of a given environment. It's important to be able to connect with other people.

As a child, I couldn't appreciate what my parents were doing; taking us out of an environment where we were comfortable and it was familiar, putting us in a completely alien environment. But it is an experience that has stayed with me for my entire life. I totally and profoundly appreciate it on a much deeper level as an adult. Learning to grasp emotionally and intellectually the complexities of humanity is important to experience early. It helps create a strong identity of self, at a young age. I believe young people should be exposed to as many languages and cultures as possible and that would help make a better, more compassionate world. Getting people to open their eyes to difference, embrace it, expands our comfort zone. We don't lose, we gain.

# Section 3
# Black English as Mother Tongue

## Black in the Day

"The American Negro has done wonders to the English language... the stark, trimmed phrases of the Occident seem too bare for the voluptuous child of the sun, hence the adornment. It arises out of the same impulse as...the making of sculpture." —Zora Neale Hurston

### A PERSPECTIVE ON AFRICAN-AMERICAN LANGUAGE

*James M., age 54, Male*
*Birthplace–Roanoke, VA*
*Occupation–Portfolio Manager*
*Mother Tongue: Black English*
*Speaks: American English*

As a Black man born in the South and educated in the North, my experience with Black English is that it is a subset of American English and the southern drawl and it has been characterized by the majority as the language of the less educated. However, I have fond memories every time I hear "y'alls" or "dats" fall out of my Grandma's mouth. It is the language of my youth. It's part of our private history—Black English—or more like a family heirloom handed down from generation to generation.

During the '70s when Hollywood made the Blaxploitation films, white directors emphasized the differences between American English and speaking hip or the language of Black America, bringing into existence a new art form: Blaxploitation films connected with Black people giving us a host of accidental heroes. Today, I see Black English used commercially in the media either as a way to show the non-black character as cool or to target Blacks for certain products.

In the late 80's while in college, I met a white fellow student who had never had a conversation with a Black person. Being very sincere, he complimented me on how well I spoke English and asked me who was my white example. Shocked, I told him that it was my parents who had taught me how to speak English. He said he thought that all Blacks spoke like the Blacks he'd heard on television. I guess he couldn't understand why I wasn't walking around saying "DYNOMITE" like the character JJ on the show *Good Times*.

I'm conscious of the multiplicity of our language in having to manage several levels of American and Black English during the course of a day. Business talk is formal, business writing is extremely formal, conversational talk with co-workers is less formal with some Black talk, but not as casual as I would talk socially with a Black friend. The last level, which is seen as the purest level of Black English is what my parents would call "slave talk," which is reserved for close friends and family.

I work at a small project management firm where our weekly staff meetings have a language component built into the agenda where individual staff members are called upon to give an off the cuff presentation in an effort to perfect our presentation skills and strengthen our use of American English. The owner is African-American. The staff is comprised of seven African-American men, one Indian, Hispanic and Black women and two white men. The Indian woman is the voice of the company (for webinars, host events, etc.) due to her perfect British accent. During the hiring process the firm's owner placed me in an informal environment then posed formal questions. My interview centered on critical points of communication, although the tone of the interview was conversational, the questions were framed in such a way that they guided me to give an impromptu presentation. The owner understands the firm is judged by the ability of the staff to speak American English, if we fail the slightest we are dismissed as not competent.

Black professionals are always fighting stereotypes even before they open their mouths. How you dress, how you walk, and how you speak are being evaluated as soon as you walk into a room. You are considered unintelligent if you don't speak English properly. I believe this is true for everyone, but more critical for Blacks because we are starting from a deficit. If I walk into a room of six people and one is white I find that the group will default to American English. I must constantly gauge the conversation of the people around me. After assessing the situation, I tend not to speak Black English though others in the room might. On the other hand, if I walk into a room where there are all Blacks talking in a Black casual situation and I start speaking American English and enunciating my words then I will be seen as snobbish or stuck up. Language affects people's relationships with other people. It dictates who your friends are and ultimately who you choose to date. The question being, can I introduce her to my boss, clients or co-workers? Understanding when it's a disadvantage or advantage to use Black English is like walking a tight-rope between two worlds.

## CODE SWITCHING: A TOOL FOR SURVIVAL

*Chandra K., Age 41, Female*
*Occupation: Playwright/Educator*
*Birthplace: Macon, MS*
*Mother Tongue: Black English*
*Speaks: American English*

*Margie: Can you tell me about your family background?*
Chandra: My family is originally from Mississippi and Alabama. Both of my parents were born in 1948 so they're baby boomers and they also lived in the segregated South. They married in 1973.

*Margie: Can you tell me how language was used in your household?*
Chandra: My great grandmother had a way of explaining things but it wasn't always explained in an articulated, educated way. Things she said would sound simple, it had a simplistic sound but the meaning was always profound. My mom and dad, considering they both grew up in rural Mississippi and rural Alabama, spoke Black English because that was the way they were raised and so as a child I grew up hearing and speaking Black English.

*Margie: So, what is Black English?*
Chandra: Black English is a language with soul in the way we go about expressing ourselves. My great-grandmother had a whole lot of different sayings, for instance she might say, "she crazy as a road lizard." I've never in my life seen a road lizard, I don't know if I'd be able to recognize a road lizard if I ever did see one but when we would hear her say this we knew whoever she was talking about was outta her damn mind. Black English is different from standard [American] English because it's not so linear and one dimensional. It sounds ignorant and uneducated but that's according to what the Eurocentric standards are for the English language. It's a language just for us because we get it, we understand it, it's the way we communicate with each other. It sounds simplistic too but if you start digging down to the root of what is being said it's actually quite profound. Blues music is a lot like that and so is hip-hop.

*Margie: So what are your experiences speaking your mother tongue in a multicultural society?*

Chandra: My experiences speaking mother tongue in America have taught me that I had to learn how to communicate to different groups of people. I absolutely sound different depending on what group I'm talking to. For example, I attended a predominantly white college and university so when I would respond to questions and participate in class discussions I knew that I had to speak in standard [American] English instead of expressing myself as I would with friends and family. I learned later on in my life that this is called *code switching* so I have learned how to be fluent in code switching where I will make a point to say *th*at, *th*is, and *th*ere instead of *dis*, *dat* or *dere*. If I'm talking to white people or even Blacks from another country I tend to speak standard [American] English so that they can understand what I'm saying.

*Margie: How have you helped someone else with mother tongue or another language?*

Chandra: One of the things in working with my students is that they live in a community that is blighted, neglected, predominantly Black, and heavily crime ridden. So it's a poor urban stricken area. My students speak their mother tongue which is pretty much what all Black English sounds like. When I am teaching children especially in this school I show them the strategies for code switching just so they can manage in this society. For instance, I was working with a fifth grader on his reading fluency and we were reading sentences out of a corrected reading book and the sentence was: Will you go to the store for more fish? He read the sentence as: Will you go ta tha sto' fo' mo' fish? I had to say, "Ok, at home you'll say, will you go ta tha sto' fo' mo' fish but at school and in the world you say, "will you go to the store for more fish?" It was about giving him tools and the ability to understand that there is a difference in how you speak to your family and friends and in your hood as opposed to how you speak when you're presenting yourself to other folks like at school or work.

Code switching is a part of life for Black folks in this country. It's part of that double consciousness that W.E.B. Du Bois talked about where you have to have a Black mentality and then you have to have another mentality in order to function in this society. I learned about code switching while I was working on my Master's degree in education because my focus is on what I like to call educational overhaul, which is really educational reform. I'm a big educational reform person particularly in the area of curriculum development recognizing cultural and learning differences. This nation being so diverse we can't afford to teach one way and think that everyone for all of the cultures represented are being educated properly. I think Black children have led the way in showing that there is a difference in the way we learn, the way we pick up on information. I picked up on code switching because it is a way we can teach black children. I didn't know that was what I was doing but after hearing an actual term for it I got deeply engrossed in it and thought yes, I can absolutely use this as a tool to teach black children.

It's about trying to keep the misperceptions down too. As a Black person in the world talking to white folks and I say that because this is where we're at, there is a judgment that is placed on you because of how you speak. There are even some Black folks who are heavy on respectability politics who have a problem with Black English. They tend to look at it as a mark of ignorance instead of seeing it as another form of communication. I see it as another form of communication and not as a mark of ignorance because you can speak perfect English and still be ignorant. So for me it's about seeing that these kids get a fair shot and we don't give up on them because of the way they sound.

*Margie: Why is speaking mother tongue important to you?*

Chandra: Because it's part of my culture. It's part of my upbringing and heritage. It's who I am and I don't ever want to be disconnected from who I am. This is not to say that if I speak standard [American] English everyday I'm not Black. Especially with me being a writer, I'm allowed to have access to all facets of language and that's empowering to have all of that at my disposal. I don't know how to communicate in just one way: I have several ways to communicate. As an artist I want to be able to focus on those aspects of Black English that everyone else has written off.

*Margie: What is your attitude towards people who do not speak English well?*

Chandra: I don't feel uncomfortable or insecure when people speak their native tongue around me. As a matter of fact I wish I knew their language so that I could talk back to them.

*Margie: I'm going to end the interview now is there anything you'd like to say on or off topic before I turn off the tape?*

Chandra: Yes. Slang and hip-hop has pretty much taken over the way we communicate in this country. Because it's so mainstream you're starting to hear white folks use words they would have never used before which are part of the Black English lexicon like "dope," "my bad," "and you know what I'm sayin'." On the one hand it's looked upon as being ignorant but once they put the right marketing spin on it everybody starts speaking it.

## IF BLACK ENGLISH ISN'T A LANGUAGE, THEN TELL ME, WHAT IS?*

*Elnora B., Age 65, Female*
*Occupation: Entrepreneur*
*Birthplace: Tallahatchie, MS*
*Mother Tongue: Black English*
*Speaks: American English*

*Margie: Do you reject or accept the idea that there is a language called Black English or Ebonics and if so why, or if not, why not?*
Elnora: I accept the notion that there is a language called Black English. I know that Blacks as a whole didn't have the same amount of education as English speaking people in America. For example, you know that I was born in Mississippi and so my parents and grandparents were raised as sharecroppers. My father went to the third grade and my mother went to the sixth grade.

*Margie: So, what is Black English?*
Elnora: I think Black English is a form of regular English or not typical of what we would say is the King's English. Not typical of the same pronunciations, the enunciations, and the grammatical structure. It's flavored with a lot of history. It's flavored with a lot of street jargon. It's flavored with what was passed down from the family internal to the household as well as to outside a person's address.

*Margie: How do you speak with your family versus how you speak with people of other races?*
Elnora: Let's see. Sometimes, it is a bit of a struggle. I mean I've always been a book worm. I was raised in a house with no TV so ever since I could read I've always had my nose stuck in a book. I've always loved English so I'm trying not to get off track from your question...[trails off] from the littlest girl on up I loved the pronunciation of words and I've always loved being able to express myself. I just took to it like a duck to water. So growing up I got through high school and went into the world of work. I ended up in occupations that required me to be in leadership roles. So this underpinned my way of speaking. I felt more comfortable with the way I sounded to myself and the way I was hearing other people speak. It felt natural. It felt good. It feels strange for me to speak differently than how I'm speaking right now. This has caused me problems but...

*Margie: What type of problems?*
Elnora: Well, when I'm around my girlfriends or when I'm around my family for example at a family reunion or when I'm at church like Sunday school with the ladies, if we have to speak or say something everybody stops and kind of looks [at me when I'm speaking] and I feel a little disconnected. A lot of people will ask me where am I from. I get that a lot. And some people have come out and said to me, "why are you talking like that?"

*Margie: Why do you think this happens?*
Elnora: I think this happens because they look at me and they see a Black woman so they're expecting to hear a Southern accent or they're looking for Black English maybe… When I was a really young woman I used to question people more about what do you mean but after experiencing this so much I stopped asking.

*Margie: You say that you talk differently from other Blacks. I wonder if in your head when you hear other Blacks speak do they sound different to you?*
A lot of influences are at play on this. Education level, peer group interaction, challenges and accomplishments inside and outside the world of work, income level, day to day environment, plus many other things that impact the way not only a black person, but any person speaks. I believe all humans are born with a blank slate which is impacted by everything around them starting the moment they hear their first sound, feel their first touch, and many things which make up their environment and their growth experiences from birth to whatever their age. Blacks, even in 2015, are not economically equal in this country which colors with a broad brush many of our experiences including the way we speak.

*Margie: What is your attitude towards people who speak English well?*
Elnora: That is a great question. My attitude is I can relax a bit. I don't have to catch up to where they are and they don't have to catch up with me. We can just talk.

*Margie: I'm going to turn off the tape to end the interview. Is there anything on topic or off topic you would like to share with me?*
Elnora: Yes there is. Because of the way I speak (and this is not to say I'm hotsy totsy or anything or that any I'm smarter than the average bear because I don't think so at all) I have been beat about the head and shoulders especially by other Black people. I'm going to say by Black women and Black men alike about fifty/fifty and it is a hurtful experience. It is a challenging emotional cave to be in and sometimes I do get emotional about it. I find myself always having to defend how I speak.

*This is the title of James Baldwin's classic essay written in 1979 for the New York Times. His essay added a voice of dissention to the raging debate that was taking place at the time over whether or not Black English was indeed a language.

## WE BE SPEAKIN'

*Name: Lorraine C., Age: 64, Female*
*Occupation: Poet/Writer/Mental Health Counselor*
*Birthplace: New York, NY*
*Mother Tongue: Black English/Geechee*
*Speaks: American English*

My family is from Denmark, South Carolina, Daytona Beach, Florida, and Lees, South Carolina. I come from hard working people. Mama had to stop school as a child to help support the family. She cleaned white folks' homes, cooked their meals and took care of their children. I grew up in a single parent household where I lived with one sister and three brothers. I had two older sisters, who lived on their own.

My mother spoke both American English and Black English/Geechee which is a mixture of African languages and dialects as well as Black English. Mama loved education, writing and reading and taught her children the same. Mama dressed well and felt comfortable in any social and professional setting. She knew about etiquette and she was a classy, articulate, stunning, creative, and brilliant woman who had common sense. I believe I first heard the term Black English when I was a young girl. It was interchangeable with the term Ebonics. My understanding of Black English is that it's English with a mixture of African languages, dialects and words created by African American Blacks which include the mispronunciations of some English words taken from the language of the American enslaver of Africans.

I consider Black English/Geechee my mother tongue. It is the language I was born into. I first heard the term mother tongue in high school. We're going back fifty years now but I was attending the Afro-American History Club in high school. My parents, teachers, community and my elementary school principal raised me to be proud of my African heritage. It was in high school that my knowledge expanded and I developed a life-long commitment to learning about my origins. One of my greatest teachers was Noel Irrizary, a brilliant Puerto Rican student, researcher and historian of African history. I accept the fact that Black English is indeed a language. It is a language understood, spoken and written by a group of people—a language with historical and cultural roots.

It's okay to speak Black English in social settings with family and friends. I would say it is not okay to speak Black English in a professional business environment where people are conversing in standard American English. I have often been in both professional and social situations where another Black person and I spoke both. It was a cultural means of connecting and a symbol of unity and family.

I only speak Black English with family, peers and friends. I refuse to entertain and indulge in the cultural appropriation of those who do not know the historical and cultural background, significance and nuances of Black English also referred to as Ebonics. It's a language of pain, suffering and survival.

## CREOLE MISSED ME, BLACK ENGLISH FOUND ME

*JR M., Age 23, Male*
*Occupation: College Affordability Advisor*
*Birthplace: Chicago, IL*
*Mother Tongue: British English*
*Speaks: American English, Black English*

My parents are from Belize, the only English speaking nation in Central America. It was colonized by the United Kingdom so the language is British English. The main difference between it and American English is the vocabulary choices are slightly different. For example, you would say "queue" instead of "line" or "flat" instead of "apartment." It's the academic language but the language you're going to hear spoken most often among the people is Creole which is based on different grammatical constructions of words that you find in the British English common lexicon. I see Black English as similar to Creole. It's not considered a language by many but I do consider it a vernacular and a spinoff of American English or a reclaiming of a language.

I grew up in Bronzeville which is a neighborhood of Chicago. In the same way there was a Black renaissance in Harlem one could say that there was a renaissance in Bronzeville. This is where Gwendolyn Brooks and Richard Wright were writing. This is where the influential *Chicago Defender* was first published and Sam Cooke lived there for some time. This kind of legacy still remains in Bronzeville even though parts of the neighborhood are more dilapidated than others.

So, growing up in this atmosphere walking around my neighborhood all I heard was Black English. It was a language that my parents looked down on because coming from Belize they were accustomed to hearing British English and they thought speaking anything other than that was incorrect--although they spoke Creole which was perfectly fine [Smiles]. I think having this immigrant viewpoint skewed my approach to Black English. I felt like it should be mine and I should be able to interact with it and speak it but for the longest time my parents would get really upset if I ever spoke it in the house. They would tell me that's not what you do; that's not how you speak.

It's because of this viewpoint that I never learned to speak Creole, which my grandmother speaks. I understand it when I go back to Belize but I don't speak to her in Creole. She has grown accustomed to speaking to me in English. My parents were adamant that I learn English and I guess it has helped me in school but when it comes to what aspects of my culture do I claim well that's another question. A lot of people would say I'm not really a Belizean because I don't speak Creole. At times that's really frustrating.

It wasn't until I went to college that I was around enough Black people to speak and interact with Black English. There have been times where I've seen people who are not Black kind of put on black face and say I'm going to use this voice. It's not a playful thing or used to communicate but rather it's a playing into the stigma and making fun of and a mockery of the language. I find this frustrating because I think Black English is a beautiful language on many different levels. The depth of gracefulness in the way things are communicated you don't find expressed the same way in English.

I have found in speaking with my friends from the Caribbean that my experience is common in that there are multiple languages spoken on any one island or area and so it's hard for an individual to pick one language as their mother tongue. My dad would probably say English is his mother tongue but he speaks Creole fluently; he speaks Spanish fairly well; and he understands some Chinese because of my great grandfather and there is a pretty big Chinese population in Belize. I believe he defaulted to British English because that's the language that was going to get him further along as far as education and economic advancement.

## FROM BLACK ENGLISH TO SLANG TO MANDARIN

*Crescent B., Age 18, Female*
*Occupation: Student*
*Birthplace: Memphis, TN*
*Mother Tongue: Black English*
*Speaks: American English, Mandarin Chinese*

*Author's Note: Through the course of this project I have found that young Black people today refer to what used to be called Black English and Ebonics as Slang although it shares the same characteristics as Black English.*

I don't reject the idea that there is a language called Black English. I actually think it's a wonderful thing for the Black community. But, before I had this interview I never really heard of Black English and I feel really compelled to talk about it because it sounds interesting.

We speak what we call Slang. I really like it and my family brought me up on it. I live with my mom, dad and brother. My parents are college graduates and they are very proper. They speak proper in public but at home they speak Slang. When they're around their family or friends or people they can relate to they're speaking Slang. But if it's in public like at work or something of the sort they're speaking proper.

If I had to define Slang I'd say it's a way of expressing how you feel using different words for the original words. At home I'll say, "ain't" but in public I'll say, "aren't". [Laughs.] Or I'll say, "Isn't this particularly fun?" and at home I'll say, "Don't y'all like dis?" Slang goes with my personality. When I'm in public I have to speak proper like when I'm in class but at home I can speak Slang. It's a part of being me.

If you spoke Slang in the workplace it's likely that you would not get the job, or let me say this, you wouldn't be accepted by the other cultures because they would be afraid of you. You know, the stereotype that if you speak Slang then you're ghetto. You're uneducated. So, it's better to just speak proper in these situations.

I got interested in Asian culture after my best friend introduced me to a Chinese band called EXO-M (the M stands for Mandarin). They were awesome! My school started offering Chinese classes and I thought this is a dream come true. My teacher Zhu Laoshi was amazing she taught me everything. After taking two years of Chinese it became my dream to go to China. I was turned down by the first program I applied to because they had too many applicants. I found another opportunity to study in China at the University of Memphis Confucius Institute. So I took it. My high school GPA had to be high, I had to get a recommendation letter from Zhu Laoshi and I had to write two essays. My essays needed editing and my mom is an English teacher so she made sure they were in pretty good shape. I got an email from the program that said we saw your application, we love it and you're in! I was like, "YEAH!" [shouts with joy] They asked me if I had a passport and I already did have one because I had been out of the country before with my parents. So all I had to do was get my visa.

It was a long plane ride. We stayed in China for a whole month. Our first stop was Beijing. It's very beautiful there—all of the buildings and the signs. One thing I don't like about China is the traffic. Everybody is in the street—cars, bikes and people. I was scared to cross the street because I thought they were going to run me over. [Laughs] We stayed at the Beijing Royal School for about four days. It was like a camp where we got our assignments on which province we would be staying at for our classes. I went to the Summer Palace, the Confucius Temple, and shopping. I rode on the bullet train too. We just did tourist things the first few days because we knew we would be studying the rest of the time.

I was assigned to Jiangsu where I took a language equivalency test and scored so high that I was put in the first class for advanced speakers. We had to wake up at 7:30 a.m. be at breakfast at 8:30AM and didn't get out of school until 9:30 p.m. Classes were great. My morning classes were language and writing. In the afternoon we had to exercise so we took Tai Chi. I took some calligraphy classes. My chaperone stopped me while I was writing Chinese characters. He said, "Crescent, stop, your characters have no spirit. You have to write with spirit. You're just writing. There's no life in it." I was like "ok." He told me to follow him and I did and my writing got better once I listened to him. Chinese is a beautiful culture and a beautiful language. It's like with the writing every stroke is beauty in their eyes. The Chinese are really different from us and I think being different is good.

I'm a freshman at the University of Memphis majoring in foreign languages. I'm taking Chinese and since I can do two more languages I'm thinking about majoring in Japanese and Spanish. I plan to go and get my Master's. After college I'm headed back to China. I want to teach English there. Or I could work at the United Nations as a translator or interpreter. I want to go back to China this coming summer. My teacher told the whole class that if we wanted to go to China now is the time. I'm young and now is the time.

# Appendix A: Poems

## CODE BREAKERS & TONGUE SHAKERS

### Tala Lualhati, Manila, Philippines, June 6, 1976

I am a bright star. I embody spiritual peace. My name is seldom found among the broken fragments and volcanic ash of Spanish and American vowels. Filipino names like the dinosaur will soon disappear.

My language is called Tagalog sometimes confused with tag along. It means "river dweller." As a young student, I remember being given a stamp by my teacher to carry with me at all times. It is in the odd shape of an indelible poem entitled, *Sa Aking Mga Kababata* (To My Fellow Youth). It is plastered on the walls of my mouth forever, and to this day, I believe /she who does not love her own mother tongue is worse than a beast and rotten fish.../ Tagalog swims with me to America as a rare riverine fish, toddling as a child who watches the back of her mother's head as she trails closely behind, her short legs trying to keep up with mother's long strides.

I have pasted the stamp on the tongues of my two American born children so that they can talk to my relatives back home. At times, my children's ticklish tongues cause the corners of the stamp to become unglued and when this happens they swap Tagalog for English learned in school, or the Black English lodged on their father's tongue.

My husband, an African-American, reminds me of the indigenous *Negritos*, the little black people, the hidden inhabitants of the Philippines only he is taller. He and the *Negritos* share tainted history forcing them to speak in two tongues.

## Makeda Tadesse, Addis Ababa, Ethiopia, July 22, 1966

my american born children
a son 12 and a daughter 8
are embarrassed and refuse
to speak Amharic my mother
tongue in the presence of
american friends
i hate that my children
see her as a despised old
woman whose teeth are
yellowed by the undying
ritual of coffee ceremonies
can't say i blame them much
americans are obsessed with
white teeth and are intolerant
of foreign accents and languages
after the wafting of aromatic smoke
after the obligatory blessings
after the bow with opened
palms turned up
after amen
before *baraka**
i was told by an elder
at the last coffee ceremony
it has been observed
in our family that our
american born children
go through this *phase*
shunning anything not
red, white, or blue
until they are 15 years old
where the tug of war ceases
and the children begin to form
a communal identity
forged by cultural pride
i wish that day was now
Amharic is our main power source
if it dies
if we pull the plug
we become discon
    nected from
family back
home
    church
and ethiopian politics
in the meantime
i will continue to do

what i can to keep
my mother tongue alive
as a rule when my children
speak to me at home in english
i respond in Amharic and
require they respond back to me
in Amharic—if they don't—
i am unresponsive to their wishes
it may seem harsh
but extreme circumstances
call for extreme measures
i must do whatever i can
to keep a warm place in my home
where my mother tongue thrives

*Baraka is the 3$^{rd}$ and final round of the traditional Ethiopian Coffee Ceremony. It means "bless you."*

## CHAKRAS OF REFUGEE EMBODIMENT OR 7 WAYS TO LOVE YOUR ASIAN BODY BY TU ANH PHAN

1. Remember the legs of your father
fleeing and gone; you are a seedling sprouting
upwardly to emerge from dirt
your roots sprawling for pockets of air
you have grown where sunlight pores through so
thank your *spine*
it has grounded your survival thus far
it stayed even when you unwind and
disfigure
so stay, you do not need to run away

2. Return to your mother's womb and bless the belly
that birth you, bless the breast that bred you
the hand, fingers, the palm that holds all of pain
praise the heave in your ankles, the lotus
blossoming in your knees
praise the history of your hips
love everyone's body
love everyone's queer
love the vagina, the penis
love all of your body
love how your skins stands you in front of unfriendly beings
who name you weak and slight
who name you exotic and dragonlike
let them name you; dicksmall and pussytight
accept all the names you do not need to fight

do not need to take up the spaces you exist in
return to your mother's *womb*; bare naked
reflect the abundance of your brown and black skin.

3. When the television was invented,
did you know it mostly broadcasted the news?
the news, all black-and-white
all warfare on our homeland
all black-and-brown guns pointed at our elders
the news was white death counts, black body bags
it was land mined of orange spray, the napalm of our
nature, the shrapnel of childrens' limbs, bombs bursting from
America's mouth
the news, a recurring image of rotten refugee flesh
displayed us disposable and dispossessed
always searching for a savior
even it he violated our soil and breached our bodies
we still drink his filtered water
we internalize what it means to be loved
but we know that there is no refuge that loves us
besides the power of our sun
we are *solar,* a plexus of yellow shades
we stay beaming 'til these cycles of violence dry out
for we radiate all over the earth!

4. Ask yourself, "Where is home?"
It is a place built to protect harmony?
Can it house a family?
The *heart* wants to be seen in the windows
wear it on an extended arm
for it is the organ of your music
the melody of a morning broom sweep
a dancing rice bowl of jingling jasmine
the forbidden fruit praying on the altar
the blood rush of a million rivers
beating rapidly, and also calmly
know that no one is an island
feel that the waves surround us all
believe. believe in forgiving
let life heal.

5. SCREAM OUT ALL THE VOICES
inside your diaphragm! somewhere
there are words that cannot be translated
feelings this world can never comprehend
let the truth escape
LET IT SHAKE
let it immigrate

free from the *throat*
let it fresh off the boat
HA! your accent is the birth mark of your parents
so, say f#ck the verb tenses,
say f#ck the "s" sound, the apostrophe,
the plural, the punctuation, the possessive
f#ck the oppressssssion of your tongue
AH! language is only broken
when it remains in your throat
now, shout this out:
"MY SOUND is the vibration of my ancestors."

6. Your eyes have only been opened to the slant
of this crooked land, the promise of this wicked dream
do not think that you are not enough
revisit the temples that values your vision
be mindful and meditate on your worthy breath
think, Third *Eye*
you are awakened.

7. Celebrate! Let us celebrate as kinfolk
let us not forget that our people have always
celebrated, have always found community
in cities, in confinement, camps and concentration
that is the core of our culture,
that is the crown of our body; our beauty
YES! Our beauty is a beast, Yes, our beauty is a god
Our body is the sacred of the in-between
Our existence is the spirit of all that is now.

## ESL BY ANONYMOUS

*Apple, Apple, Apple*

Tell it to me like this tongue
Has never trembled at the touch of tart and sweetness
These teeth never torn through reddened skin
Or crunched on yellowing flesh
That this fruit means nothing
If I can't name it in English

Teach this marionette mouth
The open/close of language
That my Cantonese
Means I can't speak
And that these China hands will only write
When the dust of chalk

Has stained them white
It's been fifteen years
Since I've known what my grandparents were saying

Kindergarten scrubbed away their meaning
With Magic Rub eraser
Their gunpowder tongues
Hit my ears like anger
I've forgotten the sound
Of lion dance pride
And firecracker elation

My mother pronounces the word "corn" like "coin"
Our waiter pretends he doesn't understand her
I have a pickpocket's accent
Patches of stolen sound clips
From television and silver screen
These chords play sunbaked California
With "O"s that "aww" like Southern drawl
And flash of muscular Brooklyn, verbal brawl
I am war-torn throat
Cloaked in hyphenated shawl

There is a white man on the bus
Who greets me in five languages
All Asian of some sort
My ears and his eyes
Can't tell the difference

I've told my parents I want to be a writer
They don't know what that means
I tell myself I will be a writer
I don't know what that means

I am a mask in miniature
Stuck in societal seams
Forgotten Flushing
In a gentrified Queens
There are two Chinatowns:
One for my culture
Another for my jeans
The tips of these toes
Trace the lines between

Topple me over, if only
For a side to stand on
I am an English major
My Vassar acceptance comes

Built on the same letters
As Chinese Exclusion

Milton, Shakespeare, other dead white guys
I've lost my mother tongue
For flighty father figures

These classroom walls
Curl 'round my neck like ten fingers

I have something to say
These hands shoot up like lightning
I'll never have the big words to make them listen
I crash like silent hailstorms
There are earthquakes inside me
They shake the cage of muted memory

*Apple, Apple, Apple.*

# Appendix B:
# Interview Questionnaire Guides

1. Tell me about your family background.
2. Tell me how you came to be in the United States. Provide as much description as possible.
3. What are your experiences speaking your mother tongue in a multicultural society?
4. Describe for me the difference between speaking your mother tongue in America and speaking it at home or with family members.
5. Describe for me the times you've had to help someone maybe in your community or workplace with language, either mother tongue or another language.
6. What have you done to become fluent in English or any other language?
7. Why is speaking English important especially if you live and work in America?
8. Tell me about your experience with learning a new language.
9. Why is speaking your mother tongue is important to you?
10. How does your family feel about your work?
11. What is your attitude towards people who speak English well?
12. What is your attitude towards people who do not speak English well?
13. What would cause you to lose your mother tongue
14. If you have children (or when you have children) will you teach them your mother tongue? Why or Why not?
15. This is the end of the survey. Is there anything else you would like to share on topic or off topic?

## INTERVIEW QUESTIONNAIRE GUIDE (BLACK ENGLISH)

1. Tell me about your family background. Provide as much description as possible.
2. When have you heard of the term "Black English"?
3. What is your understanding of the term Black English?
4. When have you heard of the term "mother tongue"?
5. What would you consider your mother tongue and why?
6. Do you accept or reject the idea that Black English is a language? If so, why and if not, why not?
7. Describe a social or personal situation where it's ok to speak Black English
8. Describe a social or personal situation where it's not ok to speak Black English
9. What is your attitude towards people who speak English well?
10. What is your attitude towards people who don't speak English well?
11. Do you speak with your family and peers as you would with other races? Why? Or Why not?
12. Is there anything else you would like to share on or off topic?

# References

Baldwin, James. *New York Times.* "If Black English Isn't a Language, Then Tell Me, What Is?" July 29, 1979.

Bernard, H. Russell. 1995. *Research Methods in Anthropology.* California: AltaMira Press.

Hemenway, Robert E. 1978. *Zora Neale Hurston: A Literary Biography.* Urbana: University of Illinois Press.

Hurston, Zora Neale. 1935 (copyright renewed in 1963). *Mules & Men.* Bloomington. Indiana University Press.

Kraut, Alan M. and David Gerber, Editors 2013. *Ethnic Historians and the Mainstream: Shaping the Nation's Immigration Story.* Eileen H. Tamura, "Ordinary People". New Brunswick: Rutgers University Press.

Rickford, John Russell and Russell John Rickford. 2000. *Spoken Soul: The Story of Black English.* New York: John Wiley & Sons, Inc.

Smitherman, Geneva. 1977. *Talkin and Testifyin: The Language of Black America.* Boston: Houghton Mifflin Company.

——— 2000. *Talkin That Talk: Language, Culture, and Education in African America.* New York: Routledge.

Yow, Valerie. 2015. *Recording Oral History: A Guide for the Humanities and Social Sciences.* Lanham: Rowman & Littlefield.

# Index

accents, 26, 27, 28, 30, 38, 68
Africa: Jamaican patois and, 44; religions in, 23; staying connected to, 19, 23, 34; U.S. views of, 24, 26, 28
African-Americans: as narrators, 11–14, 73–84; attitudes toward, 54; ESL and, 11; questions for, 7, 94; Spanish speaking Blacks and, 52, 55, 67–68
Afrikaans language, 24–25
Afro-Latinos, 66–67
Alice E. (narrator), 11, 62–64
Amadou D. (narrator), 19
Amatoulaye B. (narrator), 35–38
American born individuals: as narrators, 10–11, 59–71; as translators and interpreters, 11
American English. *See* English (standard)
Anna S. (narrator), 41–42
Anthony E. (narrator), 10, 62–64
Apartheid, 25

Bhutan, exile from, 21, 22
bilingual capacity: as a gift, 65; knowledge value of, 39, 49, 71; work value of, 35, 57, 64, 69
Black English: as communication form, 77, 80; assets of, 73, 75, 78, 82; narrators and, 11–14, 73–84; pressure to use, 79
Black Semantics, 13
Blackploitation films, 73–74
Blacxicana, defined, 71

Boas, Franz, 2–3
Bosnian War, 15–17
Bronzeville (IL) neighborhood, 81–82

Chandra, K. (narrator), 75–77
Chen H. (narrator), 17–19
Cheryl P. (narrator), 20–21
China, 17–18, 83–84
*Code Breakers* (Shaheed), 4
code switching, 65, 69, 76–77
Creole language, 81–82
Crescent B. (narrator), 12, 13, 82–84
Croatian immigrant community, 16–17
cultural heritage. *See under* mother tongue
culture, respect for, 14

Deta G. (narrator), 43–45
Du Bois, W.E.B., 2, 76

Ebonics, 11, 80
Education, 18–19, 26, 31, 63
Elnora B. (narrator), 12, 13, 78–80
English (standard): African Americans and, 12–14; assimilation and, 10; importance of learning, 35, 36–37, 50, 53, 54, 70; pressure to adopt, 9, 10, 20, 68; process of learning, 33–34, 35, 36, 46–47, 50–51, 53; professional communication and, 26, 74–75, 80
Eritrean-Ethiopian war, 33
*ESL* (Anonymous), 89–91

ESL, experience of, 11, 16, 18, 21, 33, 48
Evelyn M. B. (narrator), 28–32

Frazier, E. Franklin, 2

Gerber, Nancy, 3

Hairbraiding, 20
Henry O. (narrator), 9, 23
Heriberta R. (narrator), 34–35
Honduran/American communities, 31, 67
Hurston, Zora Neale, 1–3, 73

Ilias B. (narrator), 39–40
immigrants: as narrators, 9–10, 15–58; in U.S., 9; New York experience of, 46–47; uniqueness and artistry and, 69–70
interpreters, 11, 29, 52–53
interviews: analysis of, 8; author's process and, 3–7; questionnaire guides for, 93–94; taping of, 7–8
Irene C. (narrator), 32–33
Irrizary, Noel, 80
Israel P. (narrator), 11, 64–65

Jamaican patois in, 43–45
James M. (narrator), 12, 13, 73–75
Jodi N.(narrator), 23–26
John T. (narrator), 26–27
JR M. (narrator), 81–82
Juan C. (narrator), 38–39
Judith B. (narrator), 28–32

Kamala (narrator), 9, 21–22
Kamaria (narrator), 12
Kristina K. (narrator), 15–17

language: being born into, 12; brain development and, 65; in U.S., 1, 39; juggling, 36, 66–67, 74; multicultural communication and, 14, 71
Laure (narrator), 9
Locke, Alain, 2
Lorraine C. (narrator), 12, 13, 80–81

Madinah D. (narrator), 42–43
Mandarin language, 17, 83
Mary F. (narrator), 20

Mercy T. (narrator), 10, 66–70
mother tongue: comfort of, 39–40, 42; confusion about, 61–62; cultural heritage and, 25, 34, 51, 62, 71, 77; family communication and, 20, 32, 37–38, 40, 57, 61; identity and, 53, 62, 77; losing, 37, 60–61, 69, 71; roots and, 37, 43, 69; teaching children, 18, 19, 31, 47, 54, 62, 65, 69
Moussa D. (narrator), 10, 27–28
*Mules and Men* (Hurston), 1–3
music, English language, 68

narrator, use of term, 7
narrators, types of, 9–10, 10–11, 11–14
Nina L. (narrator), 11, 70–71

opportunities in U.S.: beating the odds and, 55–58; chef internship and, 24, 26; myth of, 27–28

patois, Jamaican, 43–45
Pidgin English, 12

Quinones, Myriam (narrator), 49–51

Rose D. (narrator), 40–41

slang, 13, 77, 83
Smitherman, Geneva, *Talkin and Testifyin*, 12–13
South African languages, 24–25
Spanish language, 31–32, 65, 70

Tagalog language, 85
*Talkin and Testifyin* (Smitherman), 12–13
Tamura, Eileen H., 59
tone, difficulty getting, 22
tongue shaker, defined, 15
translators, 11, 20–21, 40–41
Tu Anh Phan: as narrator, 10, 59–62; *Chakras of Refugee Embodiment*, 87–89; photo of, *see* photospread following page 58

Valencia family, photo of, *see* photospread following page 58
Valencia family, 3–4

Valencia, George (narrator), 55–58; photo of, *see* photospread following page 58
Valencia, Harold "Paco" (narrator), 51–54; photo of, *see* photospread following page 58
Valencia, Jesusita (narrator), 45–47; photo of, *see* photospread following page 58
Valencia, Jorge, passport of, *see* photospread following page 58

Vietnamese community and language, 60, 62

Woodson, Carter G., 2

Yonas Tsefaalem A. (narrator), 33–34; photo of, *see* photospread following page 58

Zhu Laoshi, 83

www.ingramcontent.com/pod-product-compliance
Lightning Source LLC
Chambersburg PA
CBHW021853300426
44115CB00005B/139